'Because That's What We Do'

A Pathway To Tribal Economic Sovereignty

by Gary Green

one Tribe's model for creating sustainable economic development, with casinos as the starting engine

PRINTED IN THE UNITED STATES OF AMERICA
Published by Penny Arcades Press, 5030 Champion Blvd. G11-401, Boca Raton FL 33496

The body of this book is typeset using Dr. Edmond Arnold's typography studies of pica line length and with CORONA as the body text and OPTIMA as the heads.

Gary Green Gaming™ is a registered trademark of Gary Green Gaming, Inc. The contents of this book, the cover image, and related trade dress are trademarks of Gary Green Gaming, Inc.

FIRST PRINTING
© 2019 Gary Green Gaming™ Inc. in conjunction with P.A. Press LLC

ISBN: 978-1-7326213-1-2

This book is a blueprint for the strategic planning of Tribe-to-Tribe economic development partnerships. While it tells the success-story of the Willapa Bay Enterprises Corporation of the Shoalwater Bay Indian Tribe, it actually is a handbook for intertribal processes to trans-form strained low-income Tribal enterprises into mod-ern successful economic engines.

Contents

special thanks to WBE Chair Mary Downs for editing and review

AUTHOR'S PREFACE

This short book is an outline, roadmap, how-to-guide, and strategic plan for one of the most successful sovereign-Tribe-to-sovereign-Tribe business development models ever created. Vastly different from the models of the large mega-casino Tribes to smaller Tribes, this is about a peer-to-peer nation-to-nation model among smaller Tribes.

A Tribally owned business is by its very existence a different kind of entity from a privately-owned business. The Tribally owned business communally belongs to the entire membership of the Tribe and its profits are for the benefit of the entire membership. Conflicts, politics, and general Tribal life often create roadblocks, barriers, and just general headaches for that kind of enterprise. Sometimes those barriers make the business fail; sometimes they heighten centuries-old conflicts; sometimes they keep the business from even starting; and sometimes the business survives and actually thrives *because of* that Tribal uniqueness.

Finding the precise formula for solving those problems is not for the faint of heart; and, frankly, is not for non-Natives or people who have no clue about life on a Rez. (In fact, if you have to ask, "what is a 'Rez'," then this is not a plan for you!)

This is the story of how one Tribe found those formulas and, more importantly, how they share those formulas with other Tribes. In fact, that kind of intertribal sharing is the historical tradition of that Tribe. Remarkably, it also is a really good story of how a small Tribe's business arm turned adversity into sustenance and continued their ancestral heritage of that intertribal accommodation, way-stationing diversity, and true détente.

It outlines how putting together the right team enables access to a network of partnerships, alliances, and resources that ordinarily would be far beyond the reach (and budget) of a struggling Tribal enterprise. It shows how the revenue from *casino gaming* can provide the fuel for scores of unrelated and totally sustainable, profitable, non-gambling Native businesses.

The players are easy to describe: **Willapa Bay Enterprises Corporation**; the business development arm of the Shoalwater Bay Tribe, a sovereign nation located in southwestern Washington State on the northwest Pacific coast. **Johnny Winokur**; A casino industry legend, from the heydays of Las Vegas, whose seemingly limitless acumen is matched only by his enormous heart and his boundless network. **The Network**; This is where the business plan & the story are personal for me. As part of Johnny's network, my company, Gary Green Gaming™ Inc., has been able to bring our team of industry luminaries and offer our personal dedication to Tribal sovereignty —far beyond gaming.

Most excitingly, this book serves as an introduction to how *any* Tribe can partner with WBE in this proven model for economic independence.

The book is organized as the background and story of how the model came to be and then, beyond philosophical and theoretical framework, this is the step=by-step scientific formula that is the story of their model and how it works.

At the end of the book, after the story is told and the outline defined, I also have shared my own outline for strategic planning; steps toward the foundation of the success model. Finally, this book is my homage to the greatness of what this Tribal business committee has created. To my friends in Tokeland Washington, for allowing me to join with you in offering these programs and especially for allowing me to share the story, I say Hiyu!

The Route to Economic Sovereignty

"Intertribal business relationships are important as tribal nations strive to become more self-suffi-cient and economically secure."
— Jefferson Keel, President National Congress of American Indians

"We have always known that each Tribe already has the elements for its own economic development engine. Our mission is to help them find and develop that engine; whether it is through casino gaming or other enterprises," explained Michael J. Rasmussen, one of the country's prominent economic and community development bankers.

With that succinct synopsis, he not only described the goal of Native economic development in general but also the business model of *Willapa Bay Enterprises Corporation* —the economic development arm of the Shoalwater Bay Indian Tribe of southwestern Washington State. Together that goal and that business model are the sacred mission of WBE (as the Tribal enterprise is known).

Rasmussen, a tall, slim, Oregonian with sheep-herding roots in Basque country, today serves as the Chief Financial Officer for WBE. He is quick to recite the WBE official mission statement proclaiming those goals:

"to find, evaluate and recommend new business opportunities" ... "to promote and enhance sovereignty, to promote Native American businesses and to protect tribal assets and investments. We strive to increase tribal economic development opportunities through innovation, growth, leadership, professionalism and financial discipline... For our Tribe; our People; our Future."

Under the leadership of Chairperson Mary Downs, WBE has translated that lofty vision into a viable and proven business model for both the economic success of her own people and, equally important, as a paradigm for nation-to-nation partnerships in business development. Very specifically, WBE turned their own failures and struggles around and found a way to share those successes with other Tribes.

For Downs, it really is a personal as well as social mission; her father was the beloved Shoalwater Bay Tribal Chairman Earl Davis —the very first Chairman of the modern day "recognized" Tribe. Mary Downs readily acknowledges that her work with WBE is a continuation of that legacy; true to one of the

5

most common threads through many Tribal cultures —respectful adherence to the heritage left by Tribal elders.

WBE's assisting other Tribes is along those same lines of acknowledging another historic Native mission; collaboration in the face of adversity from non-Natives who have tried to roadblock progress. Tribe-to-Tribe assistance is nothing new, especially given the historical neglect and treaty abuses of the U.S. Government.

With deliberately complex legal framework stifling economic growth, almost every aspect of Native economic development, even in the 21st century, is controlled by Federal agencies; and most of those agencies *initially* were created to abolish sovereign Tribes. It is, quite literally, the ultimate case of the "fox in the chicken coop".

Some of the government early programs even went so far as to sell off sovereign land; allegedly for the economic benefit of Tribal members but, in reality, as a pathway to Tribal decertification.

Among the most notorious of those U.S. Government "assistance" programs was the "Dawes Severalty Act of 1887"; an insidious law that was touted as *"encouraging individual initiatives furthering the progress of native farmers to lift individual Indians out of poverty"*. In reality, it was a cultural genocide "assimilation" of Natives into white society and a pathway to abolish sovereign lands by selling them to white speculators. It was the ultimate model of duplicity.

Under the provisions of the Act, in effect from 1887 until 1933, Native lands decreased from more than 138-million acres to 48-million acres. Incredibly, way more than half (almost 65%) sovereign lands were sold off in "tax auction" thievery schemes in which Natives were "given" land and then (not surprisingly) didn't have the money to pay taxes on the land. A pretty tidy little way to steal sovereign lands.

The Government's Office of Indian Affairs' 1892 official *"Map showing Indian reservations within the limits of the United States"* listed only 12 reservations east of the Mississippi River; the Qualla Territory of the Eastern Band of Cherokee Indians in Western North Carolina; the Oneida, Onondaga, Tonawanda, Cattaraugus, and the Tuscarora, in New York; Pottawatomie of Huron, and Isabella, of Michigan; and the Lac De Flambeau, Lac Court Oreille, La Pointe, and Oneida, of Wisconsin. The rest of the east coast Tribes had been decimated.

6

It was not until passage of the 1934 *Indian Reorganization Act* that the Dawes criminality was officially exposed (as Harvard history professor Ellen Fitzpatrick put it) as *"corruption, moral depravity, and criminal activity that underlay white administration and execution of the allotment policy"*.

Unfortunately, despite apparently good intentions *(with which the proverbial "road to hell" seems to be paved)* the replacement law still led to official policies of decertification of sovereign Tribes. The supposed "helpful" aid to Tribes in fact resulted in the Tribes being proclaimed extinct. In some cases, Tribal members living on their ancestral homeland were told that they did not exist. One Oklahoma Tribal Governor recalls from his youth, as recently as the 1950's, he was instructed in elementary school to list his race as "Caucasian" because his Tribe did not exist.

ABOVE: Notorious Massachusetts Senator Henry Dawes, architect of the genocidal act bearing his name.
LEFT: A US Government Dawes Act poster from 1911.

By Official U.S. Government statements and records there are more than 4,000 Native American tribes; but the U.S. Government only officially "recognizes" 572 of those Tribes[1]. The Government readily acknowledges that there are at least another 700+ Tribes that have genetic, historical, and cultural claims to be Indian Tribes but who are not officially recognized by the Bureau of Indian Affairs or that have been "decertified" by the U.S. Department of Interior declaring them extinct. The remaining Tribes, an estimated 100-million people, were annihilated and driven to official extinction by the American *manifest destiny*[2].

The well-intentioned 1934 Indian Reorganization Act began with the stated goals of reversing a century-and-a-half policy of assimilation and eradication. Its architects genuinely wanted to encourage and even adopt in white society many historical and cultural traditions of Native America. This "Indian New Deal" of the Roosevelt Administration, however, while reversing the devastating effects of Dawes, also had a "termination and relocation" provision added by the staunchly anti-Roosevelt congress. Fortunately, the devasting power of that provision remained *mostly* dormant as the government focused on the wars in Europe and Asia.

After the turmoil of World War II, during which many Natives —*including the legendary Assiniboine, Cherokee, Choctaw, Comanche, Cree, Meskwaki, Navajo, and Seminole code talkers as well as tens of thousands other warrior fighting troops* — joined with the U.S. Government to defend freedom[3], the decidedly anti-freedom terminations resumed. Amidst the post-war American growth, the 1953 Congress adopted a joint resolution to continue termination of Tribes[4].

Under this policy in which *"Native Americans would assume all the responsibilities of full citizenship"*, another 61 Tribal Nations quickly were "decertified" from existence by the United States Government. With that act as a basis, between 1954 and 1964, Congress passed 14 more acts that attempted to destroy sovereign Tribes.

It was not until 1970 that the termination policy officially ended, with a Nixon-pushed Congressional act to renounce the program. In a speech before Congress, President Nixon admitted, *"The termination era may appear as a unique event, a failed experiment that was soon corrected. But termination was actually an expression of the national will that the ultimate goal of government policy toward Indians was 'assimilation."*

With the end of the official termination policy, 78 terminated tribes were re-recognized by the United States government; 24 were declared extinct; 10 gained state recognition but not Federal recognition; 31 were acknowledged but were left landless. It was through this Nixon-era acknowledgement that WBE's parent, *The Shoalwater Bay Indian Tribe*, was officially recognized in 1971 under the leadership of Earl Davis.

Along with the end of the termination policy, the Department of Interior's Bureau of Indian Affairs instituted a series of grant programs, economic development programs, enterprise growth programs, and entrepreneurial programs for Tribes and Tribal members. Nonetheless, Native Americans remain, as a group, the poorest of the poor in the United States according to the statistical abstract of the U.S. Census Bureau. As Professor Robert Miller wrote in the Lewis & Clark University Law Review, *"There are very few bank branches, large grocery stores, or retail outlets on reservations, and an almost complete absence of businesses where people can spend their discretionary recreational dollars. Adequate roads and housing, clean water and sanitation, telephones and electricity are all in short supply on most reservations. Many Indian people on reservations today live under conditions that other Americans would not tolerate."*

Actual page from the 1953 Congressional Record showing passage of House & Senate Concurrent Resolution 108 for forced assimilation of Native Americans.

It is certainly no wonder that government "economic assistance" is often met with suspicion, distrust, and cynicism. This author's own decades in Indian Country dating back to

9

Wounded Knee are often nullified by my association of serving as a vice president for Donald Trump; albeit a brief association in the big picture of things; and that is a perfectly fair skepticism. White do-gooders don't have a great history in Indian Country, as driven-home by the Indian Reorganization Act.

Against this complex backdrop, it is little wonder that assistance from other Tribes has been welcomed with far less skepticism than always-ulterior-motive U.S. Governmental programs. Initially through closely-knit sister-Tribe connections, many programs evolved to Indian business alliances, "buy Native" campaigns, and even Inter-Tribal Economic Development Treaties.

With the phenomenal economic success of some tribal gaming enterprises, much of the 21st century Inter-Tribal assistance has come from the highly-successful gaming Tribes (the Seminole Tribe of Florida, the Chickasaw Nation of Oklahoma, the Connecticut Mohegan Tribe, The Viejas Band of Kumeyaay Indians, San Manuel Band of Mission Indians, Oneida Nation of Wisconsin, Forest County Potawatomi Community, etc.). Many of those "deals", however, more resembled the "credit-worthiness" requirements of commercial bank loans rather than true Native-to-Native enterprises.

There were almost no peer-to-peer small-Tribe-to-small-Tribe programs. Mary Downs and her board at WBE have created the much-needed "next step" in Tribe-to-Tribe economic development. A small Tribal enterprise with a disquieted history of having to borrow Tribal monies for survival, WBE structured a remarkable turnaround of their fortunes and developed a system to share their successful formulas with other Tribes.

A retired school teacher, Ms. Downs and her board quite appropriately have created a *textbook model* to be emulated by small Tribes across the country. In a series of nation-to-nation partnerships, WBE not only has the formulas for economic success but the resources and partnerships to assure those successes.

The Shoalwater Bay Tribe has a long tradition and spirit of giving and sharing both with other Tribes and with the white community around their reservation. The WBE business model, then, is only a natural extension of their own culture to export their model as nation-to-nation partnerships with other Tribes.

In a stunning 2018 "proof of concept", WBE partnered with a small, 200-member tribe located on 33 remote acres in the Cascades mountain range. That Tribe had struggled for more than 18 years to build and open a casino but had been stalled at almost every turn. WBE partnered with the Tribe and in less than six months completed what had never before been accomplished.

"I wish you could rewrite history to have my arrival at WBE coincide with the beginning of their awesome journey," Mike Rasmussen mused as he recounted how in less than three years WBE turned from struggling to a proven model for other Tribes. As a venture-interested commercial banker, he came from a world of complex financial instruments for building sustainable regional economic development programs for local governmental agencies on behalf his former employers (Bank of America Community Development, GE Capital, Bank of the West, Portland Development Commission, and others). Noting that successful economic development is an expensive process often wrought with the trials and errors of *learn-from-your-failures*, Rasmussen marvels at the WBE model of intertribal cooperation.

"True economic development, with casinos as the engine!" he marveled; "the WBE board was very smart in assembling the right team and creating the right business model."

"Very smart," he repeated in genuine admiration for the WBE board; Mary Downs, vice-chair Colleen Dietl *(herself a wily Tribal elder with a more-than-solid entrepreneurial history)*, treasurer Jamie Judkins, secretary Kenny Waltman, member-at-large Jake Christensen, and non-voting member/advisor Jesse Downs (Mary Down's Harvard-educated daughter).

The business model that now allows WBE to partner with other Tribes for economic development projects is rooted, as Rasmussen accurately noted, in using casino gaming as the underlying engine for many other sustainable businesses that have absolutely nothing to do with casinos or gaming.

There were two essential events that made it possible; events driven by perceptive wisdom and by sheer luck. That allowed the creation and structure of the WBE board itself and their choice of their uber-qualified and business-connected CEO.

For a small, remote, once-struggling Tribe to be in the position to offer these partnerships is a remarkable tribute to that WBE board that Mike Rasmussen praises.

The Johnny Winokur Story

"The true genius shudders at incompleteness."

— Edgar Allan Poe, Marginalia

At the end of August 2018, Las Vegas legend Johnny Winokur stood on the floor of the Shoalwater Bay Casino, proudly surveying players sitting at almost all of the 300 slot machines in the building. He had just concluded the most successful month in the small casino's history.

"Who, ever, would have imagined that this little casino would have a million-dollar month?" he asked, adding with a broad smile, "but we did it."

That is a million-dollars net, after operating costs.

If anyone would know casino successes, it is Winokur. A second-generation "casino boss", he has spent more than 40 years in the gaming industry all over the country; and he has never had a failure. Even with that accoladed pedigree, the Shoalwater/WBE success story is among the crowning achievements in his much-more-than-colorful career.

The driving-force behind the WBE success story and business model, his alignment with WBE was no random happenstance.

"When we were looking for someone, we had decided not just to take "the leftovers"; anyone we could find who would be willing to move here. We vowed to do what we needed to do to keep the business operating until we found someone that would really work for what we needed," Mary Downs recalls of how Johnny Winokur came to be hired.

Usually when a casino figure of Winokur's stature spends three years at a small, off-the-beaten path, property it is because he is desperate for a job and on the downhill end-of-career spiral. Nothing could be further from the reality of Johnny Winokur. Years before he'd even heard of WBE, he had made several fortunes and could have retired several times. Rather than retire, he decided to pick-and-choose projects that needed his unique talents, skill set, and massive network.

He vowed to align himself with projects that were, as he often puts it, "the right thing to do". Though he doesn't list it among his criteria for choosing projects, he also requires that they be conducive to his inimitable management style.

Mike Rasmussen tells a story he heard from some community people visiting the Shoalwater Bay casino. They were curious about who was behind all the changes that they had seen in the casino; they asked where they could find the General Manager. (Johnny is actually CEO of WBE, but also carries the title General Manager of the Shoalwater Bay Casino.) One of the employees on the casino floor told the group that the General Manager was in the casino's deli. They walked into the deli looking for a stereotype casino big-shot holding court at a table and stuffing his face on deli goodies. They didn't see anyone who fit their imagined description, so they stopped a busboy and asked which of the patrons was actually the General Manager. With a genuine twinkle in his eye, the busboy told them that he would be with them as soon as he finished clearing the table. Returning from the kitchen, after washing his hands, the busboy introduced himself as Johnny Winokur.

Legendary Las Vegas casino figure Johnny Winokur on the floor of the Shoalwater Bay Casino in Tokeland Washington.

"I actually heard that from several people in the community. That's what Johnny is all about; it is a team, and everyone pitches in, no matter what their title," Rasmussen admiringly explained; "the tables needed bussing and we were short on staff that shift. What he does is just awesome."

"Because that's what we do," Winokur emphasizes when asked about that and dozens of other seemingly out-of-character anecdotes of his management style. It was a style that he had witnessed years earlier and adopted it as his own; though he had practiced it for years, he just had never formalized it as a "style".

For the massive renovation of WBE's Shoalwater Bay casino, it was necessary to close down the facility; but Johnny didn't want any of the employees to go without a paycheck. Rather than a temporary reduction-in-force or layoffs, he found a construction-related job at the casino for every employee to remain on the payroll.

More than just caring about the employees Johnny's style developed a sense of belonging, ownership, and commitment within the entire team. There was a place for everyone, regardless of their skill level.

During that remodeling, the head bartender, a slim young woman probably still in or barely out of her twenties, climbed scaffolding to lie flat on her back, Michelangelo-style, to paint the ceiling of the deli. A few months later, long after the casino had reopened, she was overheard scolding one of the maintenance workers, "there is a chip in the paint on that ceiling tile; someone needs to get up there and touch it up." She had developed *that much* attention to small details; a sense of "ownership" of *her* casino. Clearly, she had been *Winokur-ized*.

The experience of participating in a team-effort rebuilding had successfully instilled a sense of pride and ownership at every level in the property.

The depth of commitment to that ideal is readily obvious in listening to the syntax of routine conversations among casino employees. Employees refer to the casino as "MY casino"; using the "royal" majestic plural "our". That language peculiarity is indicative of how Johnny Winokur transformed an hourly-wage employee culture to a genuine team-spirit of ownership and personal commitment to the property.

That sense of ownership, especially employees and managers using "my" in talking about the casino is a surprisingly controversial stance. Some Tribal leaders in other parts of the country have complained vehemently about "outsiders" and especially white people using the term. "This is our Tribe's casino; it doesn't belong to a bunch of white outsiders. They just

14

call it "my casino" so people will think they own it and they can boost their resumes," one Oklahoma Tribal Governor proclaimed at a General Counsel meeting.

Such failure in communicating that "team" concept of employee engagement to Tribal governments is a common mistake; but it is not one that Johnny Winokur would ever make. To assure that such confusion does not develop at Shoalwater, Johnny took the extraordinary steps at staff meetings to not only define the use of the semantic but to encourage the development of that sense of pride and level of commitment to the casino, the property, and to the Tribal asset. At one recent meeting of his managers, he strongly insisted that if any of the managers seated at the table disagreed with the hands-on philosophy of taking personal accountability for every aspect of the casino, then they should consider taking a job at one of the fast-food franchises that had opened in the next town.

He then took the results of those meetings to the WBE board meetings to let them know his management strategy. Treasurer Jamie Judkins, who periodically has lunch in the casino deli, has independently observed the change-in-attitude among employees from before-Winokur to after-Winokur. Equally important, the change in employee feelings about their jobs and about the business impact how the customers feel about spending time at the property.

"When they changed the whole casino, everybody's attitudes changed too. This place didn't used to be this friendly. Everybody is so helpful," described a woman who said she lived in nearby Aberdeen Washington, 30 miles away (and the birthplace of grunge-rock icon Kurt Cobain) and had been visiting the casino twice a week since it opened.

Winokur's commitment reaches far beyond the use of words or bussing dirty tables. He has eliminated two entire layers of casino management that are almost always in place at other casinos; Directors and Managers. A throw back to his *old-Vegas* days when management was concentrated on the casino floor rather than in executive suites (as it is in most casinos today), he has CSM's (Casino Shift Managers) filling multiple roles that in other casinos might be shared by security managers, slot managers, F&B managers, facilities managers, and others. More than a throwback, Johnny's actions demonstrated his character.

While insisting that his existing managers are as hands-on as he is, he also enforces his belief that frontline employees are the key to the success of any operation and do not need a figurehead manager; especially in a small to mid-sized operation. At any given time, Johnny himself can be found on the casino floor moving machines, in the parking lot with a bus, inventorying restaurant supplies, helping with a promotional drawing, clearing tables, cleaning ashtrays, or straightening chairs at slot machines. He expects and gets that same level of commitment from his management team, even if they don't carry the noble titles of some of their peers in other casinos.

That is the management style that impressed Rasmussen. In fact, it impressed him so much that the venture banker now routinely wades ankle-deep into the murky oyster beds he and Winokur created for another WBE business venture.

The oyster farm is just one of the WBE ventures made possible using the casino as the economic engine to drive development. As CEO and CFO, respectively, Winokur and Rasmussen oversee the casino, the oyster company, the *Tradewinds On the Bay* motel (about a mile from the casino), a convenience store, real estate developments, a small shopping strip building, a liquor store and smoke shop, a casino-related restaurant, and a bar. Other businesses opportunities are routinely evaluated.

Some inherited legacy businesses revamped by Winokur and others created specifically from the casino economic engine, the Winokur-led WBE business model creates a template for modern businesses.

The oyster business, for example, was launched from Michael doing a detailed P&L analysis of that type business before his arrival; one of the historically and culturally ties of the Shoalwater Bay Indians to their homeland. With a few advanced management controls and Johnny's unique partnering ability, the new oyster business itself has become a model for creating non-gaming Tribal enterprises from revenue generated in gaming.

It is Winokur's no-nonsense shirt-sleeve approach to every business issue that has driven the WBE turn-around. He is often heard saying, *"I am just a boots-on-the-ground guy"*; but those who work with him have learned that his decades of business experience and leadership are both intricate and complex.

The folksinger Woody Guthrie wrote that *"any fool can make something complicated, but it takes true genius to make it simple."* By that definition, Johnny Winokur is a true genius. Time and again throughout his career he has tackled complex tasks that have baffled managers, owners, and operators; and without exception, he has simplified those tasks to their simplest terms achieving results that had been elusive to everyone else.

Raised in Las Vegas, business and gaming were present in his life almost from birth. His father was the legendary Las Vegas boss *"Little Sammy"* Winokur; the man who ran some of the most famous classic casinos and hobnobbed with the fabled characters of Las Vegas history. He was long known as Meyer Lansky's personal friend. He had his own entourage of "guys" that kept casino operating smoothly even in the face of all the historical adversity and drama of Las Vegas. And, like his son in later years, he had a well-deserved reputation of one of the most "stand-up" guys in the business.

Johnny's own career includes stints as a boss at iconic Las Vegas casinos like *The Dunes, Arizona Charlie's, The Tropicana, The Aladdin, The Sahara, Silver City,* and *Pop's Oasis.* Over the years he answered to a cast of colorful bosses including Tony "Ape Head" Torcasio, Ernie Primm, Chicago trucking magnate Major Riddle, reputed mobster (and Wayne Newton partner) Ed Torres, Jimmy Hoffa's lawyer Morris Shenker, and other well-known movie-fodder Vegas names. He grew up with a roster of friendships that are instantly recognizable to Las Vegas history buffs: Teddy Binion; Moe Dalitz; Lefty Rosenthal; and dozens of lesser known peers or older associates of his father. Though he left Vegas decades ago, he is still trustee of his father's estate and home inside the Las Vegas Country Club.

Like his father, he was able to move in those circles because all of those characters *needed* a "stand-up" guy whose integrity was incomparable and whose veracity was beyond question. They needed a "boots on the ground" guy who would see to it that the operation was always clean, straight, legitimate, in legal compliance, and that the assets were always protected. That was exactly what Johnny Winokur was and is.

His huge heart, though, also shaped Johnny's career. He personally operated one of Las Vegas' best-known and most successful charities, the *"Opportunity Village Association for Retarded Children"* which earned the distinction of "Las Vegas' Best Nonprofit Organization" in the Las Vegas Review-Journal's Best of Las Vegas Awards. When asked why a leading casino boss rolled up his sleeves to set up a retail store and operate the day-to-day minutia of a charity, Johnny gives his stock reply, *"because that's what we do."* And, he means it.

17

Eventually, Johnny's lust for operating successful businesses brought him to a series of entrepreneurial projects. Among his eventual holdings were a night club and Las Vegas chain of bars with video poker machines. After turning those into successful businesses, he sold them all and accepted an offer from former Sahara Casino boss Lynn Simons, who was struggling with operating a riverboat casino under the then-new Mississippi casino laws that allowed gambling only on riverboat casinos.

Simons was operating the SS Nantucket, the last steam-powered ferry in regular operation on the East Coast of the United States. Renamed the SS Naushon, the boat was moved from Massachusetts to Greenville Mississippi where it operated as the *Cotton Club Casino*, one of the first casinos under Mississippi's new laws. Winokur's operation proved so successful that publicly-traded Alpha Hospitality bought the boat and operation trying to cookie-cutter what Johnny had created. It was a case of being too successful for his own good, since he was not an owner of the project.

Almost simultaneously, hotel magnate Barron Hilton contacted Johnny asking for his help operating the new Hilton riverboat casino slated to open in New Orleans. Johnny's unique combination of Las Vegas casino experience and now riverboat casino experience was a rare commodity in those days.

Johnny accepted the offer and jumped into the operational side of the highly-publicized fray of questionable dealings between Barron Hilton, Louisiana Governor "Fast Eddie" Edwards, Eddie DeBartolo Jr. (former chairman of the San Francisco 49ers), and their controversy of opening a casino in *The Big Easy*. It was not a pretty fight; but Johnny was the "boots-on-the-ground" guy that assured the integrity of the operation and helped assure its legitimacy.

Berthed at the Poydras Street Wharf and accessible through the lobby area of the Hilton Hotel, the Spanish Plaza, and the Riverwalk Promenade, Johnny's casino proved to be one of the most profitable and well-run casinos in the country; surpassing many Las Vegas casinos in operational efficiency. True to that "boots on the ground guy" philosophy, Johnny ran Hilton's *Queen of New Orleans Riverboat Casino* so flawlessly transparent that it passed the intense scrutiny that came with the 34-count racketeering indictment against Governor Edwards related to awarding casino licenses. In fact, Johnny's operation was so strict, clean, and open that it became the archetypal standard for casino boat operations everywhere.

That, too, is a hallmark of the Johnny Winokur business methodology; that unyielding integrity and transparency inevitably becomes the bellwether by which other operations come to be measured. Whether casino operations, business modeling, charitable functions, or opening his rescue-shelter for abandoned and neglected horses, Johnny inevitable sets the bar for everyone else to reach for its level.

The headline-garnering Louisiana upheavals further served to establish Johnny's industry reputation as a "standup guy"; the highest level of trustworthiness in the face of immeasurable turmoil.

As his reputation soared, more and more casino owners approached him to bring his skills into their operations; but none enticed his sense of helping-where-needed. None struck him as a *"because that's what we do"* project. Then Konstantinos "Gus" Boulis came knocking; and a month later Johnny was building the largest fleet of gambling ships in the history of the world — a fleet which Johnny would operate for a dozen years.

Sixth-grade dropout Boulis was a Greek national, born in n Macedonia around 1949; only two years older than Johnny. While Johnny was cutting his teeth in the gambling halls on the Las Vegas strip, Gus was traveling the world as a mechanic in the Greek merchant marines. Bored with seafaring life, he jumped shipped in Nova Scotia and worked his way to Toronto through a series of odd-jobs. Once in Canada's largest city, he blended into the Greek community there and took a job as a dishwasher in a sandwich shop which was part of a small Ontario chain.

With inexorable ambition, the dishwasher soon approached the owners of the shop with the idea of franchising their business, hoping that they might reward him with a franchise operation of his own. He presented them an entire business model description, which they liked so much that they made him manager of one of their stores, rather than an owner; but they did offer him stock in their company. He was also assigned the task of proving his franchising concept and in less than five years he had opened more than 200 franchised stores. At the age of 25, the elementary school dropout and jumped-ship dishwasher became a multi-millionaire from his stock shares in the chain.

At the ripe old age of 30, Boulis decided to retire to sunny south Florida, leaving the business world and Canadian snow behind. The move happened; but the retirement never did. Instead, Boulis decided to start his own sandwich chain in Florida. It too became a smashing success and he decided to expand his empire by buying a dilapidated tourist hotel in Key Largo, just south of Miami.

Rehabbing the *Edward – G. – Robinson -Humphry - Bogart* vision of a hotel into a viable tourist attraction, it occurred to Gus that the fledgling resort could thrive if it was attached to casino. In short order, he learned that Florida laws prohibited casinos; he incorrectly assumed that since the Seminole Tribe of Florida operated a casino, anyone could but other hotel owners had not thought to do so. Once he understood gaming law, he realized that in international waters there were no laws and no regulations regarding gambling.

To take advantage of that situation, Gus bought a small seaworthy ship and made plans to operate an onboard casino once the boat hit the high seas. A day-trip excursion, as an amenity to his hotel, if it was successful, he envisioned a fleet of "cruise to nowhere" ships that would travel the three miles offshore to international waters and open the casinos for gamblers. He reasoned that Florida's 100-million annual tourists were an ideal market for the venture. Boulis assigned his right-hand man, another Toronto-bred Greek named Greg Karan, to find and hire the best casino boat operator in the country. That, of course, led him to Johnny Winokur.

Karan and Gus' nephew, Spiros Naos painted a picture of a hapless immigrant who needed Johnny's help; the exact kind of scenario that tugged at Winokur's heart and business sensibilities. Spiros dropped Johnny off at the boat and told him that Gus would meet him soon.

In the meantime, a sweaty dirt-encrusted worker was loading boxes onto the boat and asked the waiting Johnny to help him move some of the heavier ones. *"Because that's what we do,"* Johnny pulled off his tie and jacket and spent the next couple of hours sweating with the would-be longshoreman loading the boat as he waited for the clearly-tardy Boulis. During their labors, the longshoreman and Johnny made small talk and the worker asked Johnny all sorts of questions about the prospects of success for their employer's vision. The always-transparent Winokur, between heaves and grunts as they lifted, freely shared his knowledge of what it took to make a floating casino successful and how to choose successful slot machines.

20

With still no sign of his potential employer, the two men finished loading just as Spiros returned to the dock alone. The sweating worker looked at Spiros and instructed, *"you were right; I like him. He's a worker. Hire him. Pay him whatever he wants."* The "longshoreman" was Gus Boulis and Johnny had just been the recipient of his own shirt-sleeve management style in a precursor of a scene he would replay many times (albeit with the roles switched).

For the next 12 years, Johnny worked by Gus's side and built the fleet to 11 casino ships employing more than 2,000 people; the largest exclusively gambling fleet in the world. Under Johnny's leadership, the company thrived, pulled in millions of dollars every week, and significantly increasing the fortunes of Boulis and his team, including Johnny Winokur and extraordinary gaming manager John Mollica (another day-to-day operations guru with a long history in the industry).

Though the offshore gambling scheme was completely legal, the business model irked Florida law enforcement, which constantly sought ways to shut down the fleet. Eventually, law enforcement officials found what they believed was a way to force Gus out of business; enforcement of an obscure maritime law that required American-flagged ships be owned only by American citizens. Boulis had purchased some of his fleet before he was granted citizenship. Rather than close down, the wily Boulis found a buyer for his fleet and his business; with the proviso that Johnny's value-generating management formula continue. Under the proposed deal, Gus secretly would keep a 10% stake in the company, through a proxy strawman.

Unfortunately, the $147.5-million buyers were disgraced (and soon-to-be prosecuted) Indian-gaming lobbyist Jack Abramoff and mob-connected former Atlantic & Pacific Mattress Company president Adam Kidan. In one of the most colorful and oft-told tales of 21st century casino intrigue, the sale was wrought with duplicity, corruption, and fraud; including forged bank documents, complicity of at least three members of Congress, and threats from the Gambino crime family. The subject of at least two movies, numerous books, and television shows; ultimately Kidan, Abramoff, and all three Congressmen went to prison for their roles in the transaction. Johnny's friend and boss, Gus Boulis, was gunned down in his car on the streets of Fort Lauderdale by Gambino Family soldiers.

Eventually, trial evidence showed that Gus, 51 at the time, was shot to death by a mob hit man as he sat in his car.

"I thought they were going to kill me too," testified an eyewitness who was driving home from buying milk when pe pulled behind a BMW driven by Boulis. He testified that a car suddenly stopped in front of Boulis; "There was no stop sign there. No animal or person crossing the road. There wasn't really enough space for any of us to back up and go around," he told the court. He continued recounting that a black Mustang pulled up to the driver side of Boulis' car and its driver fired several shots at point-blank range. "He pulled out a gun and shot the guy in BMW. I saw a gun over the door handle, the door frame," the testimony concluded.

Other witnesses testified that Anthony "Little Tony" Ferrari and Anthony "Big Tony" Moscatiello, reputed members of New York's Gambino crime family had killed Gus. "Little Tony" testified that another conspirator. James "Pudgy" Fiorillo, was the hitman and that Kidan was behind the plot. Kidan, on the other hand, testified that both Ferrari and Moscatiello had confessed the crime to him. Fiorillo admitted surveilling Boulis and throwing the murder gun off a Miami Beach bridge but said he did not shoot Boulis.

Kidan had ordered that Little Tony be put on the SunCruz payroll as a "food and beverage consultant". Johnny recalls being told to pay Little Tony $37,000 for the service of putting on a Super Bowl XLIII party in Tampa. Winokur remembers paying a total of around $100-thousand for the party; a party that he later was alarmed to discover never happened, despite the hefty price tag.

ABOVE LEFT: The entrance way to the Hilton Queen of New Orleans Riverboat Casino during the Johnny Winokur heyday there.
ABOVE RIGHT: Gus Boulis at a blackjack table on one of the SunCruz ships that he and Johnny created.

Big Tony, meanwhile, was given a hefty company retainer to serve as a "security consultant" but was more recognized as Kidan's personal bodyguard. Both Big and Little Tony, as well as a host of other unusual expenses, were paid by Johnny (who kept detailed records and copies of emails from Kidan and Abramoff instructing the disbursements.

Among many other media recounts of all the drama, the murder was depicted in the 2010 Hollywood movie *"Casino Jack,"* which starred Kevin Spacey as Abramoff and Jon Lovitz as Kidan. In early summer 2018, Big Tony won an appeal for a new trial.

Johnny Winokur's under-the-radar and behind-the-scenes trade mark integrity and unyielding transparency as a hands-on operator, not only kept him free of the entanglements; and his routine archiving of all emails and other correspondence provided invaluable documentation for the FBI's investigations. Once again, the model of squeaky-clean boots-on-the-ground veracity, Johnny kept the business operating free and clear of all the intrigue —and in this case homicide.

Out of loyalty to the Boulis family, Johnny stayed with the company through all of the turmoil and rebuilding following a subsequent bankruptcy. Once the company was back on solid ground, due mostly to Johnny's operational prowess, he acknowledged that he had enough.

As the wealth-generating operator of multiple successful projects, the amalgamation of Johnny's adventures had left him wealthy enough that he didn't need to work. Once again, he considered retirement. Clearly with this latest traumatic adventure he had his fill of background controversaries while he generated millions of dollars revenue.

As he weighed options, Johnny began talking with a former competitor in the "cruise to nowhere" business; a competitor that Johnny operational expertise had driven out of business. The former competitor was running a small Native American casino remotely in the northwest corner of Washington State; just about as geographically far from South Florida as possible in the continental United States; almost 4,000 miles away. The struggling casino needed an operations director; a de facto operator and Johnny —*of course*— felt that a helping hand was the right thing to do; because, well, because *"that's what we do"*.

During the next eight years, in addition to shaping the direction of the operation, he established a mentoring program for Tribal Members; developed, installed, and deployed a business intelligence system; organized numerous annual golf tournaments and charity functions; started a dealer training school; and instituted trust, guest services, manager training, public speaking, and team building programs (including Peter Scott's *"Competitive Edge"; "Train the Trainer"* by Robinson & Associates; and the *Dale Carnegie Team Building* courses.

During those eight years, he moved the casino operation to a full-fledged business development. By that time, Johnny realized that he had brought the property as far as he could, by adding the tools, training, and inspiration to operate without him.

About the same time, one of the casino's vendors told Johnny about the Shoalwater Bay Casino, a troubled property 150 miles away, in the southwestern corner of Washington.

In a short biographical sketch of any character as colorful as Johnny Winokur, it is impossible to convey the depth of knowledge, hands-on expertise, and number of expertise disciplines that he has acquired over the years.

In the face of the most tumultuous operational roadblocks in casino history —*the dicey roots of Las Vegas, the political plotting of New Orleans riverboats, the cold-blooded assassination of Gus Boulis*— Johnny consistently remained the one guy tasked with keeping things operating, keeping things legitimate, and protecting line-employees along with the public from the behind-the-scenes raucousry and turmoil.

More than a walking compendium of successful solutions to every imaginable operational scenario, Johnny himself explains it as merely a necessity. "When one of the ships *(for SunCruz)* leaves the dock, you have to make every decision; there is no other option. Whether it is catching cheaters, accounting for funds, solving crises, resolving disputes, counseling employees, or piloting the boat; there is no one to call. You have to learn what to do and you have to make the right decisions," he sighs almost dismissively and adds, *"because that's what we do."*

When asked how long he plans to stay with WBE, he dryly answers, "Until we are finished".

ABOVE: Johnny Winokur at his desk at Shoalwater Bay Casino with the nameplate at the front. **BELOW:** Johnny's nameplate with his *"Do whatever it takes"* mantra.

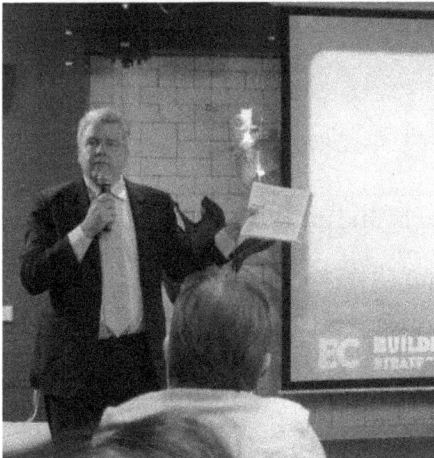

Economic development guru Michael Rasmussen leads a planning session exploring transformation of failed models into sustainable solutions.

Always Cut A Salmon Lengthwise

"If the savage resists, civilization, with the Ten Commandments in one hand and the sword in the other, demands his immediate extermination."
— **President Andrew Johnson, address to Congress 1866**

President Andrew Johnson was no friend of Native America. In fact, he is widely perceived as one of, if not *the*, worst President ever. *(Though in more recent times, that may be somewhat debatable.)*

Nonetheless, as the handwritten 1866 note at the right shows, he did set aside the reservation for the Shoalwater Bay Indian Tribe.

Probably more to keep the isolated group separated from the rest of the country on a mere one square mile of land, like many of the activities of his administration, his executive order went mostly unnoticed. Apparently, he did not even bother to notify his own Indian Bureau of the new reservation to be under their jurisdiction.

Ten years after that Presidential declaration, the Indian agent in Puyallup wrote in the 1876 Annual Report of the Commission of Indian Affairs:

"This reservation is situated on the Pacific coast, and on the north side of Shoal Water (sic) Bay, about seventy-five miles southwest of this place.

"It was set apart by Executive order of September 22, 1866. But its existence as an Indian reservation was unknown to any officer of the Indian Bureau in this Territory till I accidentally discovered it a short time

26

before the abolishment of my office as superintendent of Indian affairs of this Territory, and my visit to it last month was the first visit ever made to it by any officer of the Indian Bureau.

"It consists of about 340 acres, about one third of which is good agricultural land, but it is mostly heavily timbered, and unimproved. I found but two families on the reservation, that of the chief and his brother, each of whom has a comfortable Indian house and small garden, which is all the cultivated land on the reservation.

"About 60 Indians belong to this reservation, or rather they reside in that region, and all live by gathering oysters for the San Francisco market, which is mostly supplied with oysters from Shoal Water Bay. They are much exposed to whisky and the low vices of the whites.

"About 50 met me at the reservation and were much pleased to learn that the reservation really belonged to them; a matter about which they before had doubts. Thirty heads of families asked to be allowed to take claims on the reservation and promised as soon as their lots were laid off to settle on and improve them.

"I appointed a head chief and a council of three sub chiefs and sheriff to keep order among them, and to try to punish for drunkenness and other offenses. Having no civilizing or Christianizing influence among them, of course there is no progress in that direction with them.

"If their reservation was abolished they could not be induced to leave there, as they have no other mode of living; but there should be something done to rescue their children from barbarism and train them up in civilization."[5]

Native author and historian Vine Deloria Jr. (most widely known for his book *Custer Died for Your Sins*) noted that "it remains a mystery how the government in Washington set aside an Indian reservation without informing its officials that such a reservation existed, let alone how a reservation could be in existence for ten years before being discovered. But such mistakes were commonplace in the years when the reservations were being established."[6]

Notwithstanding the epoch-typical paternal racism of "rescuing" children from "barbarism", the neglect from the U.S. Government was probably not a bad thing. Governmental attention, historically, has not been good for Tribes.

Besides, the Shoalwater Bay Indians have a long history of independence and thriving in the face of adversity; from both the government and from nature. Only six years after setting aside their reservation, the U.S. Government sold off a portion of their reservation —without discussing it with the Tribe. Fighting back through the government's own court system, the Tribe finally prevailed; but it took 118 years. How is *that* for the Tribe's perseverance?

With an indominable spirit to survive, history has shown that it has been impossible to subdue or defeat the Shoalwater Bay Indians; no matter what has been thrown at them by man or nature.

A few hundred years ago, members of the Willapa Chinook, Lower Chehalis, and Willapa Hills Tribes banded together on the little sliver of land they called Nukaunlth (or nú?qawn̓t in the traditional Chehalis language) —named for a rough snag of driftwood that jutted into the bay. Anthropological and archaeological evidence indicates that the culturally diverse band survived through shellfish and oysters, in contrast to many of their ancestors in nearby areas who were primarily agrarian.

Until 9:00 pm on January 26, 1700 the little community was a thriving and relatively undisturbed shellfish village. On that night, without any warning signs, they were hit with a megathrust earthquake that would have measured more than 9.2 on the modern Richter scale (by comparison the devasting 1906 San Francisco earthquake was a 7.7.). The quake triggered a tsunami that ran along the Juan de Fuca Plate near Vancouver Island as far as 620 miles south to California and triggered shipwrecks as far away as Japan. The tiny Shoalwater Bay tribal village was wiped out.

Only without historical perspective were the massive quake and flooding unique events. In the bigger picture, the area has been hit with such massive quakes and flooding with a relatively consistent pattern. Researches have traced megaquakes in the area as far back as 600 BC. About 430 years later, in 170 BC, there was another; followed 570 years later by a third in 400 AD. In another 410 years the area was rocked with the massive 810 AD quake, then 390 years later the 1310 quake; then this devastating 1700 (318 years after the previous one).

28

Averaging a megathrust earthquake every 436 years and with a range of 318 to 570 years between the events, anytime between 2018 and 2270 is in the predictable danger zone with 2136 being an odds-makers prediction of the next deadly event. No longer passively uninformed, the current Tribal Council has been actively preparing early warning and survival plans for the inevitable next event. In fact, just since the 1866 Presidential Proclamation, the little town of North Cove, on the west side of the Reservation, has mostly disappeared into the ocean

What, then, might seem like *"Chicken Little"* and *"the sky is falling"* to an outside casual observer, in reality is absolutely historically prudent; and completely consistent with the irrepressible resilience of the Tribe. After the annihilating 1700 mega earthquake, the Willapa Chinook, Lower Chehalis, and Willapa Hills people returned to rebuild their Tribe and continue their heritage. They reclaimed their land, reinstated their shellfish harvesting, and began, again, to flourish.

More than 150 years after the devasting earthquake and 15 years before the Johnson Executive Order, the Smithsonian's Indian Agent, James Swan, reported a once-again thriving Native village at Shoalwater Bay. As historian Deloria wrote, "the little reservation that had existed on its own most of the time, engaged in a substantial oyster trade[7]".

Swan described his 1852 visit to a house in the village:
"Near the house was a large lodge, owned by an old chief named Toke, who, with his family and slaves, had taken up their abode, although his own place was across the Bay, at its south side, near Cape Shoalwater, at a point known as Toke's Point, a name still retained by Captain Alden on his chart.

"Toke had been a man of a great deal of importance among the Indians but advancing years and an inordinate love of whisky had reduced him to being regarded as an object of contempt and aversion by the whites, and a butt for the jests and ridicule of the Indians. But, when the old fellow was sober, he was full of traditionary tales of prowess, and legends of the days of old.

"He was also one of the best men in the Bay to handle a canoe, or to show the various channels and streams. His wife, Suis, was a most remarkable woman, possessing a fund of information in all matters relative to incidents and traditions relating to the Bay."[8]

Toke's Point became known as Toke's Land, and today is the town of Tokeland Washington.

It was not until ten years after that Johnson proclamation that the Superintendent of Indian Affairs officially appointed him as the first chief of the Tribe; under the white-given name of "Chief Light House Charley".

After he drowned, the appointment document was simply endorsed over to his son, "Go Nice Charley" to take over as the second "recognized" Chief.

"Go Nice" ran a fishing band that used an ancient netting technique called "seine hauling". A large net was draped over the side of a canoe; weights on the bottom of the net held the bottom to the floor of the bay. As the boat moved along the bay, it scooped up fish (or anything else) that came in contact with the net. During spawning season, the salmon population was so great that many times the seine did not even need a boat; the net could be simply stretched and dragged along the bay or, more likely, the shore of the Columbia River. In land seine fishing, the population of salmon was often so massive that it took an entire team of men and sometimes horses to haul the weighted nets to back to shore with the catch.

ABOVE: A very worn copy of the original Superintendent of Indian Affairs document proclaiming "Light House Charlie" the first "Head Chief" of the Shoalwater Bay Tribe.

The life cycle of a salmon begins and ends in a gravel bed in the upper reaches of a stream or river; the spawning grounds where eggs are safely laid in the gravel. Once they mature, they migrate out to the sea and undergo a series of changes shifting them from freshwater to saltwater fish. Four years later they return in mass to the same freshwater beds where they were born.

It is on that return trip, September through November when thousands of fish are traveling together, that the Tribe's nets captured so many fish.

In addition to running the lucrative fishing band, the Chief acted as guardian of 28 families, instigated work projects for the benefit of his people, and made sure the children of the Tribe were properly educated.

During many of the heavier-harvest salmon years, the Tribe was embroiled in a series of disputes with non-Native fishermen encroaching on the fishing rights of the Tribe. At times erupting into physical confrontations and at other times in a series of lawsuits. In every case, the Tribe was the rightful owner of the land and waters in question; but "right" historically has rarely been a factor between white businesses and Indians.

By 1934 the white fishermen had a new tool: the diabolical deceptions of the otherwise well-intentioned Indian Reorganization Act. Finally succeeded doing what earthquakes, tsunamis, disease, and anti-Indian schooling had failed to do.

A year later, in 1935, George Allan Go Nice Charley drowned on a fishing expedition, just as his father had. At 75 years old, he was fishing alone with a dip net at the mouth of the Quinault River when a giant breaker swept him out to sea.

ABOVE: Chief George Allen "Go Nice" Charley (center in vest and white shirt) and his seine-haul fishing crew at Willapa Bay

Despite the loss of their Chief, the pending "termination", and the land allocation schemes, the Shoalwater Bay people refused to abandon their land and their traditions. Consequently, they continued to live around Willapa Bay and existed as one the very few formerly Federally recognized Tribes which did not treaty with nor otherwise kowtow to the United States Government. As such, it took another 30 years for the Federal government to officially close the book on the neglected little Tribe.

Refusing to abandon their land and traditions, the Shoalwater Bay Tribe withstood the earth's most decimating assaults; the sea's gnawing erosion; residential schools; dispossession; an 80-acre-per-family allotment plan that actually required members to denounce their ancestry —a scheme that was later cited in a 1931 lawsuit as "evidence" that Tribal members had no claims to their ancestral fishing rights[9]; and repeated disease plagues —as recently as 1998, eight of every nine pregnancies on the reservation ended in a miscarriage or stillbirth and records show that from 1988 to 1992, at least 10 of 19 pregnancies had ended in miscarriage or stillbirth[10].

As late as 1997 the courts were still hearing fishing rights cases between the Shoalwater Bay people and land encroachers; ultimately the Tribe was denied their ancestral livelihood. Through it all, the Shoalwater people survived and thrived as people if not economically. They continued their open-door welcoming of travelers, visitors, and other Tribes. They also withstood the termination.

In 1971, under the leadership of Chief Earl Davis, Mary Downs' father, the Tribe jumped through all the required hoops and once again became a "recognized" Tribe.

No fishing rights, no farmland at all (even though nearby land provides the majority of the cranberries bogs for the USA), and no prospects for a viable social economic development plan; still these remarkably resilient people stood by their heritage and remained on their land. They remained true to their ocean culture.

In the time of Chief Toke, and before, there was a Chehalis legend told of a personified south wind arriving at the home of a giant to demand food. The giant told the wind that there was no food, but he could go fishing for some. The south wind threw out a seine net and in no time at all captured a whale.

As the wind drew his stone knife to kill the whale, the giant warned, "don't use your knife; use a sharp shell and slit him down the back. Do not cut him cross ways!" The wind pretended no to hear; he cut the whale across the back anyway.

Suddenly the fish turned into a giant Thunderbird and its wings darkened the sun; their flapping caused the earth to shake as he flew away. The wind and the giant began following the massive bird; a trip that took days and a trail up high mountains.

One day as they were gathering berries near the summit of a mountain when they came upon the bird's nest, filled with eggs. The giant cracked open one of the eggs, but it was not eatable, so she tossed it down the mountain side.

Before it reached the valley below, it turned into an Indian. She threw other eggs down the mountain and each one turned into an Indian. That is how the Chehalis people were created.

Since that time, the legend said, northwestern Indian people never ever cut the first salmon across the back; if they did, it might mean the end of their people. It might mean the salmon would no longer run. It was widely taught that one should always cut a salmon lengthwise.

THAT is how tightly bound the old Chief's people were to fish. That is how much that life was part of their culture.

Along with nature's incessant assaults on the Shoalwater Bay people, the thievery of their fishing rights *should* have been the final blow to decimate them and drive them away from their lands forever. But these people have a heritage, legacy, and birthright of resistance, endurance, persistence, survival, strength, determination, and refusal to abandon.

Not only do they remain on their battered ancestral lands, but they are unbending in their cultural heritage; especially the intertribal diversity and focus on survival that first brought together members of the Willapa Chinook, Lower Chehalis, Willapa Hills Tribes, and others. Tribe-to-Tribe economic development is nothing new to the people of Shoalwater Bay; in fact, it is historically who they are.

Section 17

"After freeing the Indian from the shackles of government supervision, what is the Indian going to do: leave that with the Indian, and it is none of your business."
— **Carlos Montezuma (Yavapai) quote c. 1916**

A Tribally owned business is by its very existence a different kind of entity from a privately-owned business. The Tribally owned business communally belongs to the entire membership of the Tribe and its profits are for the benefit of the entire membership.

Make no mistake about it; Tribally-owned or not, a *business* is a commercial activity; but except for some mechanical operational structures, that is where the similarities end.

The Oxford English Dictionary's entry for "business" takes three pages of the massive fine-print multi-volume reference. Amid all of that, the etymology of using the word "business" as a noun —*as being a "thing" rather than the activity of keeping busy*— only begins about 1350 A.D. and is strictly European in origin.

Repositioning centuries of intertribal trade and commerce to a "business" is a thoroughly white European assimilation activity; a passive cultural imperialism.

On the other hand, furthering economic prosperity amongst Indian nations —*especially coming from a Tribe that has a history of intertribal relations*— is a VERY native activity; it is very Indian.

With their rich tradition of intertribal commerce development Willapa Bay Enterprises has created both a structure and a proven model for 21st century initiatives. But like most things in Indian Country, the roadway to this mountaintop has been neither smooth nor clearly marked; there were a lot of stumbling blocks along the way.

Tribal elder and WBE vice-chair Colleen Dietl recalls the days when small Tribes like hers depended on grants for most Tribal services, including housing and a community center. With her business expertise and skill at navigating bureaucracies, she had become a formidable grant writer; but she readily acknowledged that grants were survival tools and certainly not paths to prosperity.

At that time, the main sources of revenue on the reservation were the meager private-enterprise earnings of fishing and small bingo games; and not on a Tribe-wide level. The idea to explore Tribally-owned businesses was presented to the first modern-era Chairman, Earl Davis, Mary Downs' father.

Describing him as a "most savvy" Chairman, Colleen reminisces his listening attentively and asking, "is this best for the Tribe?"

No surprise to anyone who has lived on a Rez, that hierarchal structure soon became embroiled in long-standing family rivalries and Tribal political friction. Those conflicts, which Colleen aptly terms "family hatreds", eventually led to the dissolution of that first board; as is often the case for boards and committees structured that way. The very structure made it impossible for a business to function, because any business created by the Enterprise Board was doomed to be subjected to the same political turmoil.

There was nothing unusual, unique, or exceptional about that outcome. It might even have been predictable. It certainly was a situation often repeated across the country in almost every Tribe that organized business in that model (though there were a few notable exceptions).

Like with many Tribes, for the next few years economic development was nominal, at best. Enterprise revolved around individual private businesses *(some legal and some not-so-much: fishing, quick-shop food pantries, fireworks, roadside stands, cigarettes, privately owned bingo and slot machines, alcohol sales, etc.)*; grant-sponsored development and short-term funding *(such has the ANA programs —Department of Health & Human Services' Administration for Native Americans)*; and primarily, mere survival.

Colleen, herself, developed a reputation as a successful entrepreneur, operating a number of businesses —including slot machines.

Two Congressional events shook up the Tribe's economic horizons; a land settlement act and the Indian Gaming Regulatory Act.

The land settlement was an act of the United States Congress that paid the Tribe $1,115,000 restitution for stolen lands[11]. Though the reservation was established by President Andrew Johnson on September 22nd of 1866, six years later (in August of 1872) the U.S. Government sold a portion of the same land to a private individual.

For the next 118 years the Tribe challenged this encroachment until it was finally settled on September 28, 1984. The 98th

Congress of the United States ceded the land to the heirs and assignees of the white people and paid the Tribe the cash[12].

The second impactful Congressional Act was the 1988 Indian Gaming Regulatory Act (IGRA) which acknowledged sovereign Tribes' right to operate casinos. It also set up a Federal regulatory framework for those casinos. The act, though clearly not giving any new rights to Tribes, codified their existing rights by establishing a Federal regulatory agency which provided tacit encouragement to hundreds of Tribes to open casinos for economic development purposes. Tribes across the country had been watching the developments of the Cabazon of California, the Seminole of Florida, and the Pequot of Connecticut in their legal struggles to operate high-stake bingo and casinos.

Many smaller Tribes, like Shoalwater Bay, had flirted with bingo, poker rooms, and slot machines but operated them only as a fringe activity; uncertain of how or when Federal or State authorities might react. In California, state authorities had raided the Tribe with a SWAT Team and military-invasion tactics while in Florida the entire process had been through the court system and in Connecticut it was entirely legislative. Other state and local governments were waiting to see what Federal action would be taken; and that left many Tribal operations in a sort of "Twilight Zone" of not-knowing what would happen to their gaming businesses.

On many reservations the Tribal Government avoided the issue the same way many State Governments did; leaving operations in the hands of private enterprise rather than Tribal enterprises. That was the situation that had precipitated Colleen Dietl to become the operator of her own mini-casino. It was only after the passage of IGRA that the role of law enforcement was clearly defined, and sovereign rights were both acknowledged and limited.

Together, the two Acts (the private land settlement and the IGRA) opened doors for the Tribe once again to examine establishing an *effective* enterprise board; one free of Tribal political and family complications. More importantly, the Tribe began to move toward a need to manage *resources* rather than managing social programs. The possibility of prosperity, rather than mere survival, was very real.

Typically, when Tribes tackle the issue of business management they have a complex shopping list of decisions to make; some uniquely Tribal and others just decisions that need to be made when forming any business.

On one hand, such decisions are a simple checklist; but more complexly, that checklist carries some specific Tribal eccentricities. In making decisions about how to move forward with business operations there were a number of factors to consider on that checklist:

TRIBAL SPECIFIC

☑ Preservation of tribal assets;

☑ Protection of sovereign immunity; structure for enforcement of contracts or agreements

☑ Separation and allocation of governmental powers (Exclusion of / protection of business from Tribal politics);

☑ Create an environment in which Non-Tribal investors /partners will feel secure

GENERAL BUSINESS

☑ Tax liabilities;

☑ Transparency of corporate information;

☑ Structure most conducive for:

☑ Creditors,

☑ Investor and joint venture partners, regulators, and

☑ Customers.

☑ Flexibility of managing;

The single most-critical factor in organizing a Tribal business entity is insulating the business from political interference. Establishing a managing *board of directors* and a corporate charter that is beyond the direct control of tribal council members sounds like a simple step; but those steeped in life on the Rez know better. Since all the enterprises and their assets belong to all Tribal members, it is often a huge step to say, *"you own it, but you have no control of it"*.

The very concept seems like a non-sequitur absurdity. In Tribes where one faction, one clan, one community, or one family outnumbers the rest of the Tribe, there is a certain logic to members of the majority group demanding their majority control of the assets. At the same time, that thinking also creates what sociologist John Stuart Mill famously called *tyranny of the majority* and often subjugates minorities to second-class positions.

There is a sadly infamous anecdote of an Oklahoma Tribe that operated the most economically successful casino in their casino-crowded state; at that time netting about $26-million a year and enabling the Tribe to pay each member a per-capita. A highly impugned Tribal election brought long time rivalries head to head. One side used casino resources to campaign; the other side demanded the casino business model change. Amidst it all, the Tribal Council debated, to no avail, setting up an organizational structure to shield the businesses from the tumultuous political process. When the votes were counted, the victor took control of all Tribal businesses, installed himself as casino general manager, upped the salary from $150-thousand-per-year to $450-thousand, paid off the mortgage on his off-reservation home, and —no surprise here— the enterprise began losing about $750,000 a month. Per caps were long gone and soon casino customers began to defect to other Tribes' properties. Almost twenty years later, the casino has never been profitable since.

Such examples are extreme, but unfortunately not so rare. *The Harvard Project* found that tribally-owned enterprises that are insulated from political interference are about four times as likely to be profitable as those that are not[13]. How that is accomplished, however, is an entirely different mater.

Some Tribes have successfully insolated business from politics by establishing dual governments; a traditional cultural-based government and a constitutional BIA-approved government. Others have passed constitutional amendments to establish business entities.

Still others have been less formal and have simply chosen a standard business model, established a managing board and corporate charter beyond the direct control of tribal council members, and impervious to board member removal without specific cause (usually malfeasance only). That solution is completely effective and when properly explained can remove the uncertainty and fear of risk from potential non-Tribal partners, investors, and vendors.

For the WBE, Shoalwater Bay Tribe chose the latter; once again appointing one board member from each of the four dominant Tribal families, but with the addition of one outside board member. While the board is Tribally appointed, removal cannot happen without cause.

With the organizational method nailed down, the only remaining issue, then, becomes choosing which business structure makes the most sense for any given Tribal enterprise(s). The following chart outlines the most common structures and examines the pros and cons of each.

Organizational Structure	Pros	Cons
Tribal Government. Many tribes simply create an economic development committee to handle all Tribal businesses. These usually have a separate board but not a separate legal structure. In some cases, there is no separate board; the manager of each individual business simply answers to the Tribal government. **Example:** the highly successful Mohegan Sun Tribe in Connecticut operates their casino in this style with the Tribal Council hiring a CEO to make day-to-day decisions.	Tribes and their business instrumentalities organized as an arm of the tribal government are not taxable entities for purposes of Federal income tax. Sovereign Immunity.	⊗ Tribal Politics can influence the business. ⊗ Change of Tribal government may cause change of management and business direction, destroying continuity. ⊗ Assets and liabilities of the enterprise are not segregated from governmental assets. ⊗ Some transactions require approval of the US. Secretary of Interior.
State Chartered Corporation This a standard commercial corporation filed with the Secretary of State in any state. It is owned by shareholders and governed by a board of directors elected by the shareholders. Corporations are governed by the terms and conditions contained in its articles of incorporation, which must be approved by the state. *Because of the lack of sovereign immunity, there are very few Tribes that use this form.*	Very easy to set up. Limited liability for stockholders. Protects Tribal assets from the liabilities of the corporation. Can be transparent for banks and lenders.	⊗ No sovereign immunity. ⊗ Must pay Federal taxes and likely State taxes. ⊗ Cannot issue tax-exempt (MUNI style) bonds. ⊗ Totally subject to State law. ⊗ Tribes cannot qualify as an "S" corp.
Tribally Chartered Corporation. Similar to State Chartered Corporation; and by definition, a corporation has a separate legal existence as an	Avoids state regulation. Avoids state taxes. Easy to set up.	⊗ Likely Federal tax liability; the courts and the IRS have not made a final determination.

Organizational Structure	Pros	Cons
entity distinct from its owners or shareholders. Typically, the Tribal political body retains control of the Board of Directors. **Example:** The successful Ho Chunk (Winnebago Tribe) of Wisconsin owns between a dozen and two-dozen independent businesses; each chartered as its own independent Tribal corporation.	*Possible* sovereign immunity.	⊗ Lack of transparency for banks and lenders. ⊗ Sovereign immunity is not absolute and, in some cases, can be penetrated.
Tribal or State LLC An LLC has the advantage of limited liability like a corporation. However, it is generally taxed like a partnership or other "flow-through" entity.	Generally, carries the same benefits of corporation chartered in a state or by a Tribe. Operating Agreement does not need be filed with the State or made public; unlike a corporation.	⊗ No sovereign immunity for State LLC. ⊗ Same limitations of the two corporate structures (above).
Section 17 This is a Federally-chartered corporation that is defined in Section 17 of the 1934 Indian Reorganization Act (and is copied in section 3 of the Oklahoma Indian Welfare Act). A Section 17 corporation is wholly owned by the Tribe but is legally separate and distinct from the tribal government. Nonetheless, the Section 17 corporation retains all of the privileges of the Tribe itself, including sovereign immunity. **EXAMPLE:** Many Tribal governments that have chosen to protect their business entities from the Tribe's own political intrigue have chosen the Section 17 structure.	Sovereign immunity. Even where there is a limited waiver of sovereignty (such as with slot machine leases), the law protects the assets of the Tribe from execution to satisfy a money judgment. Only the corporation's property and assets are at risk; Keeps Tribal assets within purview of the Tribe. Exempt from Federal income taxes. Can issue tax-exempt (MUNI-style) bonds. Complete flexibility in how the procedural	⊗ Law is inflexible. ⊗ Law has almost no statutory definition and therefore falls in the purview of Federal courts. ⊗ A Section 17 Charter can only be revoked by an Act of the United States Congress.

Organizational Structure	Pros	Cons
	requirements are met.	
	Has 25-year leasing authority for tribal reservation lands and Section 81 approval by the Secretary of the Interior is not re-quired.	
	Contracts and agree-ments of the corpora-tion are not subject to Section 81 approval by the Secretary of the Interior.	

Making the decision from this chart is probably the most important step a Tribe can take as they begin a genuine economic development pathway.

The WBE structure is a Section 17 Corporation. This gives them all of the sovereignty and status of the Tribe, while shielding them from the standard liabilities of many commercial businesses. They are in fact an extension of the Tribe itself but are shielded from the day-to-day political intrigue of Tribal politics.

The U.S. Bureau of Indian Affairs provides a fill-in-the-blank template for establishing a Section 17 Corporation. That template makes it easy for almost any Tribe, with or without legal counsel, to establish the corporate buffer provided by the Act. A copy of that template is in endnotes of this book[14].

The decision to organize in that structure was strategically the single most important step in setting the stage for what would eventually become WBE's successes. But merely having the right structure and the right organization is only a first step. The struggles just *begin* at that point.

From worst to first

The remarkable thing about the evolution of WBE and the
model that Johnny Winokur helped create was how they turned
it into a cookie-cutter model.

"If I died tomorrow, if Mary Downs moved to China, if the
whole Board stepped down; what we have created would continue. It would work. We have turned it into formulas and place
holders," Johnny excitedly described.

"In fact, the model is so fine-tuned that we could *cookie-cutter* it to any Tribe in the country," he added.

Still, the most revealing insight for understanding the success of the WBE business model comes from watching the current board interact with each other. As they sat in a meeting
room at the Shoalwater Bay Casino, assembled to be interviewed for this book, it was evident why they were so successful.
They demonstrated all of the elements we would hope for if we
were constructing a what-you-need-to-have board.

The board is chaired by an analytical former academic who
requires even-tempered, logical thought processes. Mary
Downs' background as a teacher and her heritage as her father's daughter provide that critical base. She is simultaneously both mentoring and inquisitive; both Socratic and Di-
dactic, as authoritative figure, but also as a guide, a resource,
and a student. Consequently, she sets the complexion and com-
portment of WBE itself as a non-rash, systematic body.

The Board wants information. They want to analyze that information, discuss, it and debate it. Then they make a decision.
Every member of the board and their thoughts & opinions are
treated equally, with value, with deference to the unique expertise of each member, and with equal validity with every other
member. That is a function of consensus, not a dictate from the
chair. The board demonstrates that it functions with classic
"critical thinking" rational, skeptical, unbiased analysis and
evaluation of information.

The vice-chair, Colleen Dietl, is treated with all the traditional respect that *should* be afforded a Tribal elder; but at the

same time is not patronized by the rest of the board. In fact, Colleen's dry sense of humor leaves an outsider with the impression that she is almost amused at her lofty status. Amidst that underlying Tribal rank, she clearly is a living conspectus of concise and detailed information and experience in multiple business ventures and relationships. As such, she is able to both analyze and provide personal-experience anecdotes in subjects as broad as slot room and blackjack operations to retail sales to government agency relations to law enforcement actions to entrepreneurial procedures. Remarkably cohesive for a board of this type, she does so without condescension or arrogance; more of the board's overall air of weighing multiple possibilities before making a decision.

The composition of the WBE Board itself is both somewhat unique and, as Mike Rasmussen noted about WBE generally, very smart. In addition to the chair and vice-chair, who are both of retirement age, the majority of the Board members are a generation or two generations younger; and as such, they are contemporarily connected to the current day-to-day vibrance of the Tribe.

This allows Board discussions to meld the seasoned experience of the older members with the contemporary experience of the younger ones. This allows both broader viewpoints and a more thorough evaluation of business matters that will impact the entire Tribe. It is the perfect example of Native tradition of melding elders' wisdom and youthful passions.

Treasurer Jamie Judkins brings an out-of-the-box perspective to WBE discussions; by her own description, she looks "at things through a different lens than most". Part of that comes from her on-going service on multiple collaborative boards (*WBE, Aberdeen Revitalization Movement Board,* and the *Pacific County Economic Development Committee*). But much of it comes from her own broad base of experience at multiple levels within organizations; from hotel and casino catering to Tribal grant writing to event coordination to enterprise planning, to earlier line-employee cashier and delivery jobs.

She combines that diversity with the discipline of her accounting education (and certification) to allow focus on organizational processes. Her narratives, questions, and summations repeatedly bring multiple levels of analysis.

Fiercely dedicated to the Tribe, Jamie's ability to give crystal-clear analyses and thought-through opinions helps keep WBE true to its Tribal mission.

43

More of that current-generation-of-leaders perspective comes from Secretary Kenny Waltman Jr., who combines his off-Rez education with his intense Tribal involvement. On a day-to-day basis he helps runs the Tribal Recreation & Fitness Center. Chronicling at his laptop the WBE meetings, as the Secretary, gives him the unique ability to reference other Board members' thoughts when responding or providing his own input. That input typically is well thought out and most importantly assures the perspective of the Tribal mainstream.

The WBE Board keeps its hand on the pulse of the frontline on-the-street Tribal members through Board Member At Large, Jake Christensen. In the book-interview meeting as well as on several other occasions, Jake proved himself to be a pull-no-punches voice on the Board. With an obvious talent for cutting directly to the at-the-core-issue of a subject, Jake thoughtfully listens to a discussion and then frankly interjects a to-the-bone street analysis; rarely tempered. Not at all negative, his analyses and comments provide a much-needed and usually-effective perspective of potential impact of any given project.

He also has a really good handle on projecting Tribal and extra-Tribal reactions to various initiatives. He also is a "hands-on" Board Member who repeatedly shows a willingness to jump in to help with any job, no matter how messy.

For WBE to reach its current level of success, it took this unique collaboration of individuals with highly-divergent backgrounds and exceptional dedication to their people. Without a doubt, they inherited a number of misfired, dysfunctional, directionless enterprises as well as some success stories. Nonetheless, their unique composition and the collaboration of the combined skill sets is a model for other Tribes wondering how to compose their business boards.

Beyond picking up the pieces from previous management structures, this Board started from scratch in evaluating business. That also meant that they had to turn-around general Tribal perception about the business board. Both were monumental tasks.

Just as Colleen describe the unfathomable tasks of her grandfathers —*learning the white man's ways*— this 21st century board had to train themselves in the eccentricities of modern budgeting methodologies, casino "flash" reports and benchmarking, yield management, granular perspective, paradigm shits, resonance and sustainability, detecting data coloration, JIC and JIT production, and evaluating core competencies.

It also meant fine-tuning relations with the Tribal government to assure transparency but absolute independence. Driven by love for their Tribe, these Board members began cementing those principles as well as defining which tasks fall to which individuals and establishing policies to choose Board members by qualifications. By extension, those same principles applied to protecting employees and managers of their various enterprises; in part a communications process asking questions, enforcing performance standards, and holding people to those standards (as well as protecting their jobs if they performed to the standards); and shielding employees from political interference.

The processes required an intense focus on building a "team" concept, a Johnny Winokur methodology; strategic planning and goal-setting; and a persistence in following through when things got tough.

Almost none of the projects, enterprises, and businesses that the board inherited were deliberately or maliciously out-of-step; rather, for the most part, they were either out-of-date or never properly executed in the first place. It was into those murky waters that the WBE decided to dive head-first.

"You don't see that kind of enthusiasm and excitement in the banking industry," noted Mike Rasmussen as he talked about what brought him to WBE.

"This is not a job; it is an adventure where everyone's excitement comes out," he added.

"In my role as a banker and a grant writer, I had worked with a number of non-casino Tribes; and I was proud of it," he continued.

"I had heard that the Shoalwater Bay Casino was closed, and I wondered what had happened there; so, I reached out to them. This is when I met Johnny Winokur; and nothing has been the same since," he explained his arrival.

The closed casino that he described is the perfect case-in-point of the WBE process. The history of the casino inherited by this Board and their decisions of what to do about it is both metaphoric but corporal manifestation of what a board needs to be and needs to do.

The National Indian Gaming Commission (NIGC) approved a gaming ordinance for the Tribe in February of 1998 and two months later the troubles began. The issue was blackjack games in the casino.

The Tribe argued that they had been operating blackjack games on the Reservation before the 1988 Indian Gaming Regulatory Act (IGRA) passed and therefore the game should be "grandfathered" in (allowed) under the provisions of the Act.

IGRA has a grandfather provision specifically written for Michigan, North and South Dakota, and Washington State; states which already allowed card games. The IGRA provision required that the game had been played on the reservation before the Act and the game be operated by the Tribe itself.

The NIGC investigated, heard witness testimony, and ruled that the game was indeed played before the passage of IGRA; step one proven. However, the NIGC also ruled that the game was *not* conducted by the Tribe itself, but by individual Tribal members; and the games were not licensed nor otherwise officially sanctioned by the Tribe. Blackjack games, then, were deemed illegal at the Shoalwater Bay Casino in absence of a Compact with Washington State. The NIGC rejected the application for grandfathered status.

In the big picture of sovereignty, the Tribe's position was correct. Card games were legal in the State of Washington and therefore were a regulatory/civil matter rather than criminal. Even the most conservative interpretation of sovereignty provides that regulatory issues are civil matters and are subject to Tribal regulation not State regulation. If the Tribe's determination for regulation was to *not* license, then that decision itself was a sovereign nation's decision on regulation.

Nonetheless, the NIGC held the Tribe to the letter-of-the-law with IGRA and *that* provided grounds for the denial. This was one more of hundreds (if not thousands) of examples of how IGRA *took away rights* rather than granted any new rights; IGRA is a structure for Federal regulation and control and not a granting of a right to gamble[15] (as many think it is).

Almost exactly a year later, in 1999, the Tribe was again at odds with the NIGC; this time "dinged" with a *"Notice of Violation"* for operating "Class III[16]" games without entering into a compact with the State of Washington. That notice was accompanied by a *"Order of Temporary Closure"* of the casino and a fine of $27,500.[17]

The NIGC identified five slot machine titles as Class III true slot machines rather than bingo-based Class II games: *Native Treasures; Catch a Dream; Sheriff's Round Up; Pirate's Loot;* and *American Game Technology Cash Key Video.* The NIGC also said the Tribe was illegally operating pai gow poker, roulette, and continuing to play blackjack despite the previous ruling.

The Tribe acknowledged it did not have a Tribal-State compact with the State of Washington for the play of these games but maintained that a compact was not required for play of the games. While the Tribe's appeal was pending before the Commission, the NIGC agreed that the casino would be allowed to remain open and continue playing games, with the exception of *American Game Technology Cash Key Video*, pai gow poker, and roulette.

During the lengthy wait for the hearing, three-years later, the Tribe entered into a gaming compact with Washington State; in effect making the issue moot. Nonetheless, the NIGC argued that some of the prohibited games were still illegal even with the Compact in place.

In a negotiated settlement agreement, the Tribe refused to admit wrongdoing but agreed to pay the fine if the NIGC would withdraw the *Notice of Violation* and *Order of Temporary Closure*. In mid-November of 2003 (four years after the incident began), the agreement was signed by both parties. From a regulatory standpoint, this ended the Tribe's issues. Operationally, however, a long nightmare had just begun.

In sharp contrast to the sleek Vegas-style casinos operated around Seattle, Tacoma, Spokane, and other high-population centers, Shoalwater Bay Casino was a low-ceiling, smoke-filled dive designed like a rectangular box. In one of the more unusual casino design flaws, the restrooms were positioned directly at the front door so that the first thing an arriving patron saw was a water fountain (adorned by mounted heads of dead animals) and the entrance to the restrooms.

Years later, longtime casino employees explained the then-logic of the bizarre design. The casino, like many Tribal gaming enterprises, had been divided into two operations; bingo and slot machines/table games. The original design concept had been to separate the bingo players by putting that game on the southside of the small 3,000 square foot building and putting the casino players on the north side. Placing the restrooms in the middle was both convenient and provided an easy barrier between the two operations. Logical as it may have seemed, in practice it was just clumsy and ugly.

That physical obliviousness to customer perception and marketing was symptomatic of a host of difficulties; problems that might have been obvious to industry veterans but unexpected to those not seasoned in the eccentricities of the casino business. The assortment of issues combined to make for difficult times for the enterprise that otherwise should have been the *cash cow* for the Tribe. The Shoalwater Bay Casino was not that kind of success.

The uninitiated might attribute the difficulties to the remote location of the Rez. The casino is on a tiny almost-peninsular jut in Pacific County Washington, in the town of Tokeland (named for Chief Toke) and with a population of only 194 in 2000 (and down to 151 in 2010). It is 145 from Seattle; 148 miles from Portland Oregon; 85 miles from Olympia; 137 miles from SeaTac Airport; 33 miles from the closest population center, Aberdeen with only a little more than 16,000 people there. There are no interstate or four-lane highways leading to the casino. Within a 100-mile circle from the casino, there are 45 casinos and card rooms[18].

Nonetheless, many remote casinos, much more isolated, were vastly more profitable and enjoyed relatively steady business. Most of *those* casinos operated within profitable parameters and were able to provide some economic benefit to the Tribe.

As recently as April of 2015, the Consolidated P&L Statement for the Shoalwater Bay Casino showed net income as a $674-thousand *loss*; and that was not unusual.

Public perception about casinos is that they are money-printing machines; that since all the odds are in favor of the casino, casinos are a foolproof always-profitable business. Reality, however, is entirely different. As one former executive of Las Vegas' famed Wynn Resorts recently noted, *"people think casinos are like any other business; but believe me, I have been in the hotel business and the casino business they are nothing alike. Successful casinos are like nothing else; it requires a lot of specialization to make them successful. Most people don't realize that."*

Casinos are, indeed, highly-specialized businesses with very specialized metrics and business terminologies that have entirely different meanings than they do in traditional businesses. For example, that posted $674-thousand one-month loss meant that almost $8-million in actual cash flow had to pass through the casino in just that one month and more than $95-million annually. Few businesses other than casinos and banks have the procedures and metrics to deal with that much cash-flow in a month. Consequently, Federal law requires that all casino employees who handle cash must have the same certification of Title 31 training as bank tellers[19].

Title 31 is the anti-money laundering act that originally was known as the "Bank Secrecy Act" but now includes casinos. Currency transactions that occur within a single *Gaming Day*[20], whether the currency is paid into the casino, paid out, or exchanged (in the case of foreign currency exchanges), in excess of $10,000 requires the completion of a Currency Transaction Report (CTR, FinCEN Form 112[21]) and must contain enough information to accurately identify the individual(s) transacting the currency.

In fact, the law is so strict that it is a Federal crime, punishable by imprisonment, to tell customers that they are nearing reporting thresholds. It also is illegal to disclose the time that the Gaming Day ends. These are just among the basic peculiarities of casino operations.

Moreover, casino operation is an extremely formulaic business that requires highly-skilled implementation of those formulas to be successful. Formulaic and self-perpetuating as they are, setting the requisite structures and procedures for proper implementation is a highly-coveted skill set; a skill set that *should* be plentiful but definitely is not.

With more than 500 casinos in the United States and the average tenure of a General Manager less than three years, there is always a glut of unemployed GM candidates. Add to that an unimaginable number of mid-level managers seeking to move up, and the number of potential casino executives is massive.

However, what WBE and many other casino organizations have learned is that having worked in a casino (or even having run a casino) does not automatically translate to expertise or success. Shoalwater Bay, again like many casinos, went through multiple general managers without effectively turning the casino into that hoped-for economic development engine...or even "cash cow".

Then WBE met Johnny Winokur and their world changed. The significance of Johnny standing on that casino floor in 2018 and marveling at a million-dollar month is even more remarkable given the perspective of where the casino had been even three years earlier.

"I met the WBE Board, a group of really nice people who were absolutely dedicated and committed to their Tribe; but they didn't understand casino financials or negotiations," he recalls from his first meeting with WBE.

With a sigh, he continued, "They were sincere and doing the best they could do, but essentially, they were just placeholders. The Tribe was subsidizing them and, truthfully, from a financial standpoint the casino should have been closed. It was a disaster; for lots of reasons."

"We talked, and they said *Please, we need help*; and that did it for me. I didn't need a gig; I could retire at any time. But someone needed my help and they asked for it. That was it; I was in," he concluded.

Mary downs elaborated on the process, "We had gone out and had another successful GM of a local slot-only facility come out look at the place to give us some ideas to get us started to profitability. He recommended that we close down table games and Bingo; and we already knew we needed another GM. So, we did all three and then along came Johnny."

She elaborated, "Johnny heard of us and came to us. During our interviews we were determined to find the right fit and not *accept and settle* for less. We knew we needed help from someone who knew the business, would live in Tokeland, and be willing to work for the salary we could afford. Johnny was our best "bet". We had a winner against all those odds. He said yes."

"He was exactly what we needed. He has always taken time to educate the Board on the details of the business, set up reporting mechanisms so we knew how to keep track of the daily money flowing in and out. He was open to our ideas — like having the managers coming to the Board meetings so we could meet everyone, know their faces, and reassure them that we were there to support them. The Board also gave authority to Johnny to run the business as he saw fit and have been ready to back if there was any backlash."

Winokur's first step was to sit with WBE's comptroller and drill down into the finances of the troubled casino. The first thing he discovered was how far behind they were in payments to vendors.

"We owed one slot machine company $500-thousand dollars. Under the terms of the Washington State Compact, that vendor could have closed us down. That would have been the end. I called the vendor, who of course knew me and gave him my word that we would pay the balance, but I needed time and I needed to remain open. He didn't have to, but based on my personal promise, he agreed to terms," Johnny said. Continuing his examination of the books, he discovered that the casino was at least three-months behind on payments to every other slot vendor; and the casino owed the Tribe $500-thousand dollars.

"There were bad contracts, bad publicity, bad marketing, bad operations. I found that we had billboards 140 miles away; what was that all about?" he still incredulously marvels.

Calling on his encyclopedic casino knowledge and decades of operational expertise, Johnny began applying cutting-edge casino management methodologies and using advanced casino metrics for analysis as a basis for decisions.

"I was able to immediately save $396-thousand without one single layoff. That was just to get started and just by managing the right way. I was able to start paying the bills," he explained.

Meanwhile, 150 miles away, the Cowlitz Indian Tribe was planning to open a new 100,000 square foot 2,500-machine casino resort. Far outside of Shoalwater's competitive area, the Tribe was not authorized to be licensed for that many slot machines, though their feasibility study and financial projections called for *at least* that many. The Washington State Compact limited each Tribe to a base of 975 machines but allowed Tribes to "lease" from other Tribes the rights for up to 1,525 additional machines.

This unusual law allowed smaller casinos or non-gaming Tribes to lease any or all of their machine rights to larger casinos. At the then going rate, non-gaming Tribes could earn up to $4.9-million a year just for assigning their machine rights. Even more interesting, IGRA exempts Class II (electronic bingo-based slot machines) from state compacts, so leasing the machine rights only impacts Class III games; Tribes can have an unlimited number of Class II games.

Finally, the lease rate was determined free-market style, negotiated Tribe to Tribe without State interference; though there was a standard rate that most Tribes paid. Shoalwater had already leased the majority of their allotment but retained rights to a handful of games.

Johnny Winokur filed away that information about the Cowlitz' needs and continued his examination of the finances of Shoalwater Bay Casino. He became more and more troubled about the business model of the casino.

"It just didn't make sense the way it was organized; the costs were too high for what they could do in that limited space in the condition it was in," he said, admitting that he began thinking about a major remodeling for the casino.

51

Reaching into his vast industry network, Johnny called Josh Coit, the co-owner *American General Construction*, a hospitality and small-casino construction guru. Coit flew into Seattle and drove down to Tokeland to walk the casino floor with Johnny. Together the two experts outlined an optimal design for the casino, using the existing structure and resources they had. They decided it would cost around $1.1-million to completely rehab the casino and bring it into the 21st century.

"Given the financial situation, I knew I had to make a decision and make it fast. Did I want to close the casino, lease the game licenses, and lay off 100 people or did I want to do something radical," he remembers.

He met with the Tribal officials to discuss the casino's ongoing obligation to pay the Tribe a per-game licensing fee for the Class III machines. Together they explored the possibility of taking out all of the Class III games; the casino would no longer have a per-game obligation to pay the Tribe and the Tribe could lease the licenses for the 375+/- games to other Tribes.

At first the Treasurer thought Johnny was suggesting closing the casino and walking away. Johnny, on the other hand, was talking about converting the casino to a total Class II facility.

"There was resistance at first; the objection that Class II games don't do as well as Class III games. But that absolutely not true anymore. It used to be, but the new Class II games do just as well, and in some cases better, as Class III games," Johnny explained.

"Plus, the 80/20 revenue share model is a great model for a smaller property earning less than $150 per unit per day. It might not be a good idea for a large property earning $450 per machine per day; those casinos can buy a new machine in a very short period of time. But for little guys, it is the perfect model; the vendors change titles and cabinets as needed, provide parts, service the games, and I don't need slot techs on the payroll," he explained.

Vendors lease Class II games to casinos, but *almost* always sell Class III games. The going rate for purchase of a new Class III slot machine ranges from about $18,500 to $25,000; the lease that Johnny likes is a revenue share in which the casino takes 80% of the win-per-machine-per-day and the vendor is paid 20%.

Johnny was well aware that on a strict accounting IRR (internal rate of return) analysis, the decision to lease or purchase slot machines is complex. In deciding between a lease and purchase, decisions have to be made about such issues as whether the casino or the vendor will cover the costs of changing themes, converting denominations, refurbishing cabinets, changing location on the floor, marketing specific games, and dozens of other related decisions. Additionally, policy management and financial management need to figure into the determination as well as the cost of money the casino will have to pay to borrow funds to buy the machines. Then the depreciated value of the machines as an asset needs to be examined.

These are all decisions that larger casinos often employ entire finance analytical departments to evaluate. One of the remarkable talents that Johnny Winokur has the experience and knowledge base to make those calculations on-the-fly and usually in his head.

If we assume a small remote casino having a low win-per-machine-per-day of only $100 and a 20% yearly decline in win because of new technologies and other aging factors, then we can plot the IRR of a machine purchase:

PURCHASE IRR	1st year	2nd year	3rd year	4th year	5th year	Total
Price of machine	($18,500)	$0	$0	$0	$0	($18,500)
Annual win	$36,500	$29,200	$23,360	$18,688	$14,950	$122,698
Net Profit	$18,000	$29,200	$23,360	$18,688	$14,950	$104,198

Even with declining win per unit, the net profit on a machine shows more than $100,000 or an internal rate of return on the investment of 176.90% An IRR metric is standard for helping management decide if they should make an investment; it is a standard indicator of the efficiency or quality of an investment.

Where this becomes complex is when comparing that IRR to and IRR for leased games —assuming the lease terms and conditions are negotiated favorably by casino management and not just accepted as a form lease from the vendor.

"That was one of the most important points Johnny taught us, right out of the gate," Mary Downs noted.

With the right terms, the casino can require the vendor to replace the machine (without charge) whenever a new latest-and-greatest is released or whenever the machine's win per day falls below a pre-determined minimum.

Lease IRR	1st year	2nd year	3rd year	4th year	5th year	Total
Price of machine	$0	$0	$0	$0	$0	$0
Annual win	$36,500	$36,500	$36,500	$36,500	$36,500	$182,500
20% lease fee	$7,300	$7,300	$7,300	$7,300	$7,300	$36,500
Net Profit	$29,200	$29,200	$29,200	$29,200	$29,200	$146,000

From these two tables, leasing a machine actually gives the casino $41,802 net revenue *more than* buying the machines would provide. This startling revelation does not take into account the added expenses of hiring slot technicians, ordering and storing supplies and parts, and the expense of upgrading; all associated with owning machines but not existent in a lease arrangement.

The lease model provides some incalculable IRR (something like 292,000% if we posit only a token price for the casino).

The lease model, then, benefits both the vendor and the casino more than the purchase model benefits either —again, if and ONLY if management has the skills, ability, wherewithal, and experience to negotiate a contract with those favorable terms.

In short, while on the surface lease versus purchase may seem like a no-brainer, clearly the decision has such a major impact on the business model itself that the "no-brainer" becomes a complex key indicator of the soundness of the business. The decision involves performance, value, negotiations, availability of finance and cash flow options of the casino, and a headache-giving myriad of other management assessments and actions; not the least of which is the cost of money for a capital expenditure of purchasing.

Those complexities of slot management decisions are indicative of the cosmos of issues relating to how well operational management conforms to and meets the budgetary formulas established by policy management. Every venue of casino management, finance, and marketing is equally (or more) complicated as the slot decisions, though not al-ways as palpably so.

These are just small samplings of the complexities that large casinos wade through by using a dozen or more separate analysts and projection procedures. It is also a small sampling of what Johnny Winokur routinely measures in his head as he walks a casino floor.

"I made the decision to covert to Class II and not layoff one single person. I borrowed the $1.1-million from the Tribe and converted to a totally Class II property," Johnny explained.

"We closed on April 1st (2017) and on the third and fourth all the machines were out. Josh Coit and his team came in and we used the existing casino employees as the labor for the rehab. Thirty days later, we reopened with a brand-new casino," he proudly described.

Meanwhile, in thirty days, Johnny and his unlikely construction team of casino employees worked with Josh Coit to completely remodel the small Shoalwater Bay Casino. The front door in-your-face restrooms were moved and replaced with modern led-lit high-tech plumbing facilities. The two rooms were converted to a large modern casino floor. A new high-tech and interactive-LED bar was installed in the center of the casino. All new cutting-edge-title Class II slot machines were brought into the property. Additional ventilation and smoke-eaters were added. A new deli was created.

"In 30 days, we completely rebuilt, and we were back open," he proudly explained.

WBE Chair Mary Downs recalls, "we told him to move forward with his proposal but had two requirements; to be finished in 30 days and to stay within the budget. And he did it. As a Board we are truly grateful to all those people who jumped in and painted, cleaned up, dumped garbage, pulled wires, pretty much whatever was needed".

Besides transforming the building and the economic paradigm of revenue, Johnny also transformed the outlook and participation of the employees; he created that "team" that has become a trademark of his work.

"This was another trait we liked about Johnny when we interviewed him; he emphasized a team aspect," Downs added.

That is the enthusiasm that had attracted Rasmussen to the project; and that is why the casino was closed when he showed up to meet Johnny.

"I had never seen this kind of democratic collaboration that Johnny had created. And, the enthusiasm wasn't just from the line employees; it was everywhere. Mary Downs was one of the most enthusiastic people I met. All of the managers and department heads were energized," he said.

"There are three drivers of success in projects like this; we call them 'The Three P's': People, Place, and Purpose. WBE and

Johnny Winokur had brought those elements together like I have never seen," he continued.

"It is almost spiritual. There is no behind-the-scenes intrigue; none of the b.s. that I had seen in other places. This is genuine, and it is all part of that *'do whatever it takes'* attitude that Johnny brings with him everywhere," Mike added.

"This is the "funnest" job ever," Rasmussen laughed in a mock little-kid voice. Then suddenly taking a serious tone, he added, "Johnny really does believe in participatory management; it is awesome." The wry, knowing, little smile on Rasmussen's face shows genuine fascination and respect for what his boss has created at WBE.

Rasmussen started in the finance industry literally at the bottom; he worked in the basement cleaning and emptying trash. During his career he moved up to almost every conceivable job in the banking world; not unparallel to Johnny Winokur in gaming and business. During a stint with GE Capital he became a member of CEO Jack Welch's legendary legion of *Six Sigma* statistical modeling and process management experts. Along the way, he found he had a skill for economic development, project development, and grant writing, especially for non-gaming Tribes.

His portfolio includes some of the most successful Indian housing, health, and start-up business projects in the country; and his reservation experience includes living on some of the most remote and impoverished reservations in the country.

His introduction to Johnny Winokur's world is the embodiment of the modern WBE methodology. From the standpoint of an economic developer, the creation of a successful anchor — *in this case the now uber-performing revenue-generating casino—* is the ideal springboard for creating opportunity.

"The opportunities and the economic possibilities, within the Tribal environment but with the business development perspective can now be realized like never before; not just for WBE and The Shoalwater Bay Tribe, but as a template for partnerships with other Tribes," Rasmussen explained.

He added, "There are many more moving parts in this business. The pace is faster. Back to the numbers, even the productivity is greater. The attitude toward renovation and rebuilding is energizing and exciting."

"Johnny and WBE weed out the negativity. People that bring a project down are told if they don't like it, they can leave. People who remain involved in the projects take ownership and completely buy into the energy of the projects. That is part of the awesomeness of this," he added.

"The most remarkable and important element here is that there is no *bucket of crabs syndrome*. Johnny's model creates a culture where there is an urge to advance. Once exposed to the culture of winning, people find teams that win," he marveled.

The *bucket of crabs syndrome* is a sociological metaphor noting that when a group of crabs are put in a bucket, any one crab could easily escape but each time one attempts to escape the other crabs pull it back into the bucket; ensuring that they all will remain captured and eventually killed. When applied to human social behavior, it is the tendency of members of a group to reduce the self-confidence of any member who achieves success beyond the others, out of envy, resentment, spite, conspiracy, or competitive feelings, thus halting their progress. There are a number of academic studies of that behavior[22]. Mike was noting that the culture created by the WBE model avoids that negativity, which is often present on reservations and other near-closed social groups.

"This model strikes a blow against that kind of intergenerational trauma; and it is completely portable (to projects where WBE partners)," he added.

Rasmussen concluded, "this excitement is contagious. People want to be part of this; especially when they see that everyone is hands on, no matter who you are."

Johnny Winokur chimed in, "When I call it '*my*' casino, it is because everyone should feel part of it. In fact, everybody should want my job. The model should be that everybody wants to move to the next level. Everybody should be fired up with the excitement. I hope every one of my managers is after my job. That's the way it should be, and I encourage it. That is what mentoring is all about."

Many organizational leaders tout their "shirt sleeve" approach of their "hands on" approach; but few actually practice beyond a token showing. Other leaders will do limited front-line work. Very few provide the Johnny Winokur example of bussing tables, moving slot machines, pouring oyster mixtures, driving buses, and actually being part of the teams.

The partnership aspect, the portability, of the WBE business was summed up by Rasmussen as three intertwined elements:

1. The financial model of the casino; the buy-in to the structure and the culture;

2. The philosophy of renovation; the same energy and spirit that allowed the Shoalwater Bay Casino transformation in only a month can be applied to the entire ethos of partnered projects.

3. Almost unlimited economic development possibilities using casino gaming as the engine without the other businesses being part of or tied to a casino.

Those elements combine with that encyclopedic skill set that Johnny carries with him on a daily basis. They also give him the basis to tap into his seemingly endless network of experts and specialists.

For various projects he has been able to bring in Coit's *American General Construction; Barbara Davis*, one of the nation's premier hotel operators within the casino space; *John Mollica*, a seasoned casino manager, staff trainer, and teacher; and international bingo guru *Roger Ooms*.

And, of course, Johnny has access to the *Gary Green Gaming*™ organization (including, the CEO, super gaming attorney Buddy Levy, one of the founding fathers of the modern Indian casino industry and former Trump vice president Gary Green

TOP: Johnny Winokur is *"hands on"* moving slot machines during installation at a new casino for a Tribe that partnered with WBE.
BOTTOM: More *"hands on"* attitude as Winokur examines a grow pot for the WBE oyster farm business.

58

—television star and the author of this book).

The right combination of this Board, their passion, and the very existence of Johnny Winokur has taken the business model quite literally from worst to first. Moreover, it has set up a way to export their successes into partnerships with other Tribes.

Planning

Despite massive 1960's and 1970's grant programs from the Office of Economic Opportunity and other Federal and state programs available in Indian Country, there is no doubt that the creation of casino complexes (including hotels and resorts) have proven themselves to be one of THE most successful economic development programs in modern Native history.

At the same time, as WBE learned the hard way, simply having a gaming operation does not assure riches; and even having a marginally profitable casino does not mean it is optimized for the maximum profitability.

Newer generations of Tribal leadership have broken the BIA mold and come up with creative, educated, and often cutting-edge solutions for their people; often bringing in consultants, mentors, teachers, and occasionally a rare "Johnny Winokur" character (though *those* are few and far between).

WBE has been able to take their proven success from that model and make it portable for partnership with other Tribes. WBE is not a bank and they don't fund projects, though at times they can find funding for projects.

As Johnny Winokur regularly says, he and WBE are "boots on the ground". That means they are developers, operators, managers, advisors, and mentors.

As Michael Rasmussen said early on, *"We have always known that each Tribe already has the elements for its own economic development engine. Our mission is to help them find and develop that engine; whether it is through casino gaming or other enterprises"*. **That is the most succinct definition of what WBE partnerships are all about.**

The phenomenal success of the WBE model and partnerships is very systematic and formulaic. It is structured, planned, projected, and executed according to very specific direction. The process begins with very specific planning exercises; essential to develop good management, adequate financing, best use of time & resources, and the ultimate success for the Tribes involved.

Unlike planning for typical white businesses, Native businesses belong to the entire Tribe and are carried on the shoulders of thousands of years of ancestors' teachings, legends, songs, stories, and culture. An Indian business, by the very nature of its existence, has a spiritual history. A Tribal business plan comes with communal core values —non-Tribal business plans do not necessarily carry that attribute.

In that regard, Tribal business development is a "mission" as much as it is an enterprise. It certainly is a historical and cultural mission for the WBE Board.

In the planning process, those are the first things which much be defined; the underlying mission and the core values of the Tribe. What are the real goals?

Once that step has been thoroughly explored and defined, it is time to look at the viability, practicality, and probability of a project's success. This is usually done with a *"feasibility study"* which formally defines the business concept and how it will be organized.

The feasibility study examines the market demand, the people, the product or services, prices, location, and promotion necessary for success. The study develops sales forecasts or "projections" of revenue, including the sources and how that revenue will be obtained.

The study should explore the management and operational resources that will be needed and how those resources will be obtained. The collaborative exercise for this study should also determine the full organizational and personnel requirements for the proposed business.

At that point, it is necessary to estimate how much money will be needed to start the business and from where that money will come. Part of *that* process should include putting together forecasted financial statements, sometimes called a *pro forma.*

A proforma is a spreadsheet that shows projected revenue and expenses. This document is not expected to be an auditor's perfunctory GAAP (Generally Accepted Accounting Practices) analysis, but rather it is a more practical detail of how estimated projections of expenses and income are made for a new business. The pro forma is a reflection of the business *operation* and usually does not include non-recurring expenses or start-up costs; it is a financial modeling tool.

A second financial tool, equally important for this initial process, is a schedule of projected start-up costs and explanations of each.

Finally, but equally important, the feasibility analysis should include a discussion of risks of the business type and of this specific version of the business. This is usually done with a break-even analysis as well as exploration of hazards to the business.

For some extremely complex businesses (like casinos operations, cannabis operations, and others) it is often necessary to bring in third parties with expertise in the specific metrics of specialized operations. This is the most effective way to get accurate projections, likelihood for success, and very specific steps that need to be taken for success. However, even in those cases, the Tribe's business committee should be involved in the process for maximum transparency; this is a hallmark of the WBE methodology.

The economic feasibility, operational feasibility, and detailed (technical) feasibility should be carefully planned before moving forward. Again, this is essential to that planning process.

This entire process is a vital part of the partnering process with WBE. The experience of WBE shows that a true partnership has the highest likelihood for success when both Tribes are involved in this feasibility process. Consequently, that is one of the very first services that WBE brings to a new partnership; a jointly created feasibility study, beginning with fleshing out the very core business idea or concept.

Once that study has been developed and the essential questions answered, a financial plan is developed. Often this includes the creation of a balance sheet, operations statement, and cash flow analysis, all along with complete financial forecasts including detailed operating expenses.

Also, part of this process, once the feasibility study has been completed, is the decision about the form the business organization should take. *(Needless to say, WBE is partial to the Section 17 model).*

A marketing plan, at this point, becomes the next important tool for planning the business. WBE has found that the *questions* to be answered by the marketing plan are very simple:

- Who are the customers?
- For what are they spending their money?
- How much will they spend?

- Where will they come from?
- When will they spend?
- Why will they spend?

Answering those questions, however, is usually far more complex than just asking them; and each requires detailed analysis and discussion. This, too, is a collaborative process between WBE and the partner Tribe.

The next step is to create an organization chart for the new business, along with job descriptions, wage/salary/benefits details, and a policies & procedures document.

All of these steps still are part of that overall planning process. The planning itself is an exercise of engagement of the partner Tribe with WBE. Rather than being "spoon fed" the details and results of these processes, WBE insists on collaboration so that the partnered Tribe shares the sense of ownership that Johnny Winokur created with Shoalwater Bay Casino employees and managers.

The WBE Board has learned that this kind of engagement and sense of "ownership" is essential for long term success.

Once the feasibility has been determined and the decision made to go forward, it is time to prepare a business plan. A business plan of this type is a compilation document that includes:

- A concise statement of the goals;
- The market factors;
- Resources available;
- Capital requirements;
- A summary of the results of the feasibility study;
- The complete financials;
- Details and resumes of the management team and key personnel;
- … and (most importantly) how the business is going to make money (marketing).

Assembling that plan and the supporting documents is another part of the partnership process with WBE.

Once that is complete, it is time to put together a financial *package*. The purpose of this package is to convince an outside objective financier that the Tribe can operate (in conjunction with WBE) a competitive business with sufficient revenue to repay business debts, sustain business growth, and provide additional revenue for the Tribe.

In short: Is this a sustainable business that stands the test of traditional business financing?

The financial package evaluates the Tribe's potential for success in the business (specifically, how they will make it work). It determines what kind of financing the Tribe will need and what financing is available.

Most importantly, the financial package needs to be presented in a standard format as a set of documents typically presented to financial institutions; this is part of the Michael Rasmussen expertise.

The package also needs to be created with a constant focus on the cost of financing. WBE assists in finding potential financing sources, including at times some of WBE's own connections and resources.

It is clear that *strategic planning* is a good deal more than merely setting goals; it is a series of processes to create systematic and manageable implementation of the partnered visit. Once that WBE initial planning process is completed, then the work begins!

As WBE's experience has shown, success is tied to expert operations —which also includes the training and mentoring of team members.

Johnny Winokur repeats, "I cannot emphasize enough how we have made this into a template. It started with a very special team; but that team, *THAT* internal partnership, created something entirely new. We made this so that it is self-perpetuating. It does not need me; it does not need these specific people. It just needs what we have created."

The fabled Johnny Winokur with a jackpot winner on the floor of the Shoalwater Bay Casino

Willapa Bay Enterprises Corporation offers a first step toward business success to any Tribe looking for a partnership. As Johnny Winokur says, *"because that's what we do"*.

APPENDIX

bonus training section for this edition only

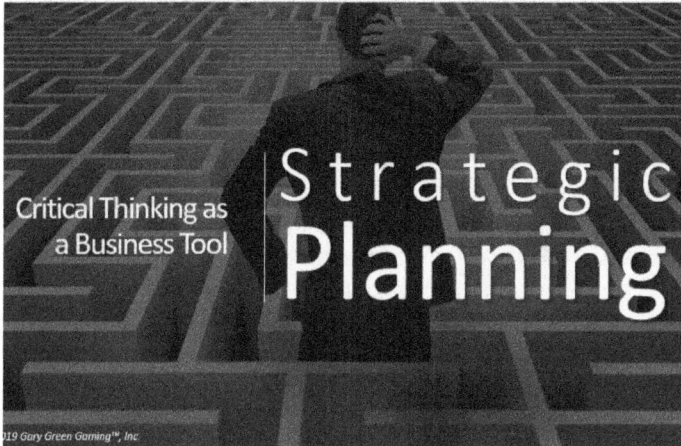

Critical Thinking as a Business Tool

Strategic Planning

019 Gary Green Gaming™, Inc.

This Appendix is a special bonus section for this edition of *Because That's What We Do*.

The book itself was written to be an introduction and guide to entering into Intertribal business relationships between Willapa Bay Enterprise Corporation and other Tribes.

A key element to making those businesses successful is the process of "Strategic Planning".

Elaborating on the lists and goals set in the final chapter of the book, this Appendix is a special introduction and step-by-step training guide for the Strategic Planning to implement the elements of that chapter.

Many business lecturers, authors, facilitators, and even government agencies offer training and exercises for Strategic Planning. Many of those lectures and trainings are incredibly insightful and methodically useful.

However, in our decades of experience, we have found that many of those trainings are impractical for implementation into the day-to-day realities of Tribal life.

Gary Green Gaming™ has a different approach to the standard elements of Strategic Planning. We have learned that the five elements of traditional Strategic Planning are excellent tools; but they are only tools.

What often is missing is a way to make strategic planning a day-to-day process as natural as breathing itself.

Our methodology is to teach the real-life skill of **Critical Thinking**. Once *that* skill has been mastered and internalized, strategic planning becomes natural and even routine.

Our focus is to teach Critical Thinking as a business tool for strategic planning.

Separate from the book itself, this Appendix is the outline we often use for that training. It is included here as a starting point to effectively implement the processes described in the last chapter of *"Because That's What We Do"*.

We begin by defining the elements of strategic planning; but we conclude by teaching to tools of critical thinking so that *all* planning routinely becomes strategic.

Strategic Planning is a sea best navigated with an experienced captain; but most organizations are not fortunate enough to have a *Johnny Winokur* at the helm.

In lieu of having your own Johnny Winokur, the following pages are offered as a study-guide introduction to those planning processes and to provide preliminary steps toward success.

As Johnny Winokur often says, *"Never failed; never will."*

> "Although some organizations may survive and prosper because they have intuitive geniuses managing them, most are not so fortunate."
>
> —Fred R. David

"The Beginning Is The Most Important Part Of The Work"
—Plato

Beginning the journey toward success, is not unlike the start of *Alice's Adventures in Wonderland*.

While in pursuit of the mystical white rabbit, who apparently was late for a very important date, Alice plunged through the rabbit hole into the new adventure.

Later, lost in her new world, the little girl turned to a wily Cheshire Cat and asked, "Please sir, where should I begin?"

The cat coolly replied, "at the beginning, of course my dear."

For us, the beginning is to ask the most-basic question, **"why do we even need a plan?"**

Planning itself provides clear direction to answer several starting=point questions for any venture:

+ "Where are we going?"
+ "How are we going to get there?", *and*
+ "How will we know if we succeed?".

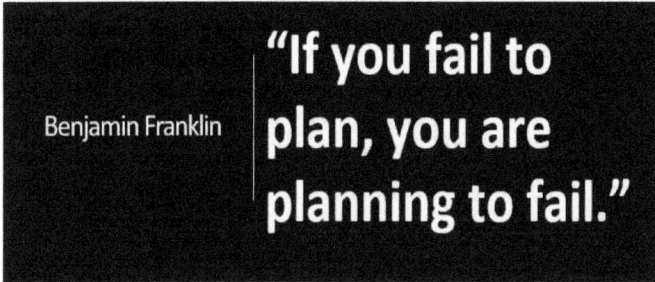

> **"If you fail to plan, you are planning to fail."**
>
> Benjamin Franklin

Adding the element of *strategic* to mere "planning" sets the expectation that we are going to identify long-term goals or overall aims and interests as well as how we are going to achieving them.

Strategic Planning gives us benchmarks to track our progress.

Strategic Planning gives us a structure for making choices about the use of our time, money, and people.

Strategic Planning helps us build consensus about goals and directions.

Strategic Planning allows us to clearly communicate unified objectives and expectations.

Strategic Planning allows us to manage effectively and to achieve results.

Strategic Planning is the process of determining what a business should become and how it can best achieve its goals.

Strategic Planning is a process to set priorities, focus energy & resources, strengthen operations, ensure that everyone is working toward common goals, establish agreement around intended results, and assess & adjust goals.

This process is essential to developing:

+ good management
+ adequate financing
+ and determining the best use of time & resources.

67

Ultimately, Strategic Planning can be the determining factor for success or failure.

A good strategic plan has five key elements:

1. Vision
2. Mission
3. Objectives
4. Strategies and
5. An Action Plan

One effective way to go through this exercise is to make lists on a white board as we detail each of these elements.

These five elements are closely related to each other and as we begin the process, they overlap and become one element.

① and ②

We begin with the elements of the VISION and the MISSION of the plan.

We need to create a simple statement of our vision; our purpose for any particular project.

We do that by answering two basic questions about the project:

+ What are the benefits of the project?
+ What are the IDEAL conditions for success?

Those answers make our "vision statement". That statement should be inspiring, uplifting, and easy to communicate. If possible, it should be one simple sentence.

From that vision statement we can define our mission. The mission answers two additional questions:

WHAT ARE WE GOING TO DO?

and

WHY?

Those are probably the most important starting questions; they are certainly the most basic.

The answer to those two questions will be the Mission Statement.

Ideally, we should be able to answer both questions in one sentence. That statement should be concise (to the point).

That sentence should be outcome-oriented and should clearly explain what we are working to achieve.

Since we are a TRIBAL mission, the statement also should be inclusive; not just a vision for the business committee but for the benefit of all the Tribe.

Creating those statements, answering those questions, is much more than just a simple list. We need to "all be on the same page"; we need consensus about the mission.

③ and ④

OBJECTIVES & STRATEGIES. Once we have agreed on that statement —through consensus— we are ready to talk about the steps to accomplish the goals we just outlined.

To do that, we need to discuss and answer another series of questions:

1. Polices & Procedures:
    a. Do we need to modify existing policies, *or*
    b. Do we need to create new policies, *or*
    c. Does the project handily fit into existing policies and procedures?
2. What are the specific steps that we need to take to implement our plan.

This is exercise is not to list the details of HOW to make it happen (*that* is the strategy). Rather, this simply is a list of what the steps are.

> For example, two of the *steps* might be "A: Manufacture The Product and B: Sell The Product". That does not detail the steps in the manufacturing process or how we sell the product. Instead, this is simple a list of the objectives.

As we answer those two questions we also need to decide if it will be necessary to modify (or create new) opportunities and (most importantly) reduce obstacles to the project.

Part of that process includes defining how we:

+ Provide information about the project;
+ Enhance our skills and the skills of the key individuals participating in the project; and
+ Enhance the services and products that we are offering.

⑤

ACTION PLANS

This gives us a starting point to create an action plan to reach our goals.

Specifically, we are ready to ask, "how do we reach these objectives?". That process is the strategy.

As a group, we collectively should list the things we believe will be necessary to accomplish our mission.

This is done by again turning to our white board. This time we will detail exactly how our strategies will be implemented to accomplish the objectives that we have developed in the previous processes.

+ First, we list the "Action Steps"; exactly what needs to happen.
+ Next, we will list assignments; which person(s) are responsible for which tasks; who will do what.
+ We will list the date that each task is to be completed; the timing of each action step.
+ On our white-board, we will list the resources that are required to omplement the plan. We need to note what is available currently and what is needed both in terms of resources and support.
+ In this Action Plan, it also is important to make note of obstacles, barriers, or resistance that we will need to overcome.
+ Finally, we need to note who else should know about our action plan; who are our collaborators or potential collaboratiors?

THAT is all there is to it; we now have an Action Plan.

DREAMS TO ACTIONS TO OUTCOMES

These six elements give us the blueprint for moving from dreams to actions and then to outcomes.

This is an on-going process designed to give us structure and direction.

It helps us build consensus about what to to and how to do it.

It gives us a tool to focus our efforts.

It allows us to accurately project what will be accomplished by when.

Ultimately, our Action Plan focuses us in three directions:
1. How we get it done.
2. Remove obstacles.
3. Make outcomes matter by increases support and recources.

These three items give us the specifics of who will do what, by when, and at what costs.

With that, our strategic plan is now complete. We have a vision. We have a defined our mission. We have listed our objectives. We have agreed on specific strategies.

We have an action plan for moving forward with the strategies we have created.
1. Vision
2. Mission
3. Objectives
4. Strategies and
5. An Action Plan

Moving Our Strategic Plan Forward

The final step in the strategic planning process is to implement our plan.

Even this is formulaic and can be outlined step-by-step.

We begin with an assessment of how things are now and a discussion of where we want things to be.

We determine our limitations, both internally and externally (this includes resources and financing).

We develop clearly-written objectives for each department to implement.

When making such decisions, it is always best to have the maximum amount of information available to us.

In assembling that information, we also need to take into account social and economic trends that might impact our strategic plan.

An effective strategic planning process, complete with benchmarks and milestones, usually takes from one to three months to complete.

That lengthy planning and evaluation period is one of many reasons that the most important tool in the process is how we make our evaluations and decisions.

Further, operating a Tribal business can be deeply personal; often filled with emotion, politics, guesswork, cultural bias, suspicion, and trial-and-error.

One shortcut to avoid a long *process of missteps and experimentation is to adopt "critical thinking"* — a technique for quickly analyzing opportunities and determining how to react to them; all within the confines of your newly developed plan.

The single most essential business tool for strategic planning is that process of critical thinking.

Business success depends on taking a cold hard look at the numbers and facts, and using that information to make choices consistent with the strategic plan we created.

One of the most difficult tasks in the planning and organizational processes —*especially for group decision-*

making— is the task of being objective. Yet, the objective analysis of facts to form a judgement is a fundamental skill for effective planning.

Critical Thinking is a way to quickly analyze those facts without jumping to conclusions from opinions, reluctancies, or fears.

The fundamental skill of Critical Thinking is the ability to weed through guesses and possibilities to almost instantly make determinations that are *guaranteed to be accurate*.

At its best, Critical Thinking is a way to make objective decisions. Developing that skill requires us to understand how conclusions usually are reached.

There are three ways that people develop conclusions to make decisions:

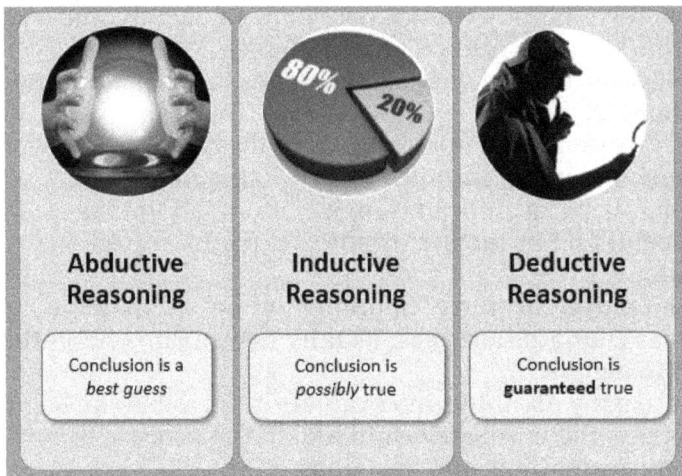

Abductive Reasoning	**Inductive Reasoning**	**Deductive Reasoning**
Conclusion is a *best guess*	Conclusion is *possibly* true	Conclusion is **guaranteed** true

1. **Abductive Reasoning** is the process in which a conclusion is a "best guess" based on available information.
2. **Inductive Reasoning** is an only slightly more accurate process of reaching conclusions. Induced conclusions are *possibly* true but are still uncertain.
3. **Deductive Reasoning** is a process in which conclusions are guaranteed to be accurate.

Obviously, the latter is what we need to learn to do. However, to develop that skill, we need to understand fully how conclusions are made using other methods and how to quickly recognize the mistakes of non-dedictove thinking.

In order to do that, let's take a look at all three reasoning processes and examples of how they work.

<u>Abductive Reasoning</u>, unfortunately, is the way a lot of business decisions are made; and, in part, why they fail.

Rather than theory or pure logic, Abductive Reasoning is a "best guess" from observation.

EXAMPLE of abduction

One prominent example of this kind of reasoning is the recent panic of the casino industry over the failure to attract gamblers from the "millennial" generation. That panic, and the business decisions based on it, show a classic example of the failure of abductive reasoning.

Observation tells us that:

+ The average of Las Vegas visitors has dropped from 55 to 40 years old.
+ Millennials make up the largest segment of the population.
+ Millennials seem to have short attentions spans and become easily bored.
+ Millennials' spend less money gambling and more of their money in bars & restaurants and on technology.
+ Observed data is that Millennials only spend 8½% of their budgets gambling, compared to Baby Boomers spending 30%.

Based on those observations, many pundits have concluded that business models need to be radically altered to address these observed changes. A number of national magazines and gaming trade journals joined the "sky is falling" bandwagon and predicted the end of casinos as we know them, unless the industry adapts to the needs of the millennial generation.

The failure abductive reasoning

A more detailed examination of data reveals faulty reasoning in creating the panic in the first place.

A 1955 *Life Magazine* article predicted the fall of the gambling industry in Las Vegas because the then-new Baby Boomer generation didn't match the gambling psychographic profile. A data comparison of that 1955 Baby Boomer situation to the modern Millennial generation reveals some interesting comparisons:

	BABY BOOMERS 1955	MILLENNIALS 2019
Don't gamble like their parents	YES	YES
Low net worth	YES	YES
Largest population segment	YES	YES

	BABY BOOMERS 1955	MILLENNIALS 2019
Highest consumer spending	YES	YES
Spend at restaurants & bars	YES	YES
Driven by technology	Television	internet
Short attention span	YES	YES
Bored easily & seek adventure	YES	YES
CONCLUSION	THE END IF CASINOS	

An examination of the facts revealed that rather than a dramatic paradigm shift in the business, there was merely a generational shift. Younger consumers, of either era, do not have the free cash to gamble. Large debt loads, interest in spending in other area, even free time; all impact the decision to gamble.

Decisions made from Abductive Reasoning are not only ill-informed but could be financially disastrous if entire business models are modified based on the faulty thinking. In that light, it is easy to see how making a decision without all the facts can be a mistake.

Inductive Reasoning is a step above that "best guess" and weighs *some* data to offer more likely outcomes.

Inductive reasoning begins with a specific proposition and arrives at a general conclusion. Even if all of the premises are true in a statement, inductive reasoning allows for the conclusion to be false.

EXAMPLE of induction

A good example of Inductive Reasoning business decision is a recent slot machine problem given to one northwestern Tribe's casino General Manager. With the best of intentions, he made decisions about what slot machines to put on his casino floor.

Here was his thought process:

+ He had experience at several casinos in Oklahoma. At every Tribal casino in Oklahoma, a specific company's "Hot Seven" slot machine title was the floor-leader in terms of win-per-machine.
+ In every casino he surveyed, that particular machine won more than $200 per unit per day.
+ Therefore, he induced, those machines would be highly successful in the Pacific Northwest at a Tribal casino there.

The failure Inductive reasoning

At the Tribal casino in the Northwest, that same machine (with the same theme and same payout) won only $14 per unit per day. It did not even make enough to justify having the game on the casino floor.

The induction was false.

There was real data on which a decision could be based. it was not a "best guess" because the game looked good; the decision was based on a real history of the game.

However, the decision took *specific information* (the Oklahoma actual data) and drew a *general conclusion* from it.

Just because something worked in some specific situations, does not mean it works everywhere. If all the kids in one room have red hair, that does not mean that all children on the planet have red hair; even if it is true that everyone in that one room did.

Inductive reasoning is better than a "best guess" and offers a "maybe" or a "probably" solution.

It does not, however, remove all opinion, guesses, and emotion from an issue.

That brings us to DEDUCTIVE REASONING.

Most frequently associated with *Sherlock Holmes,* DEDUCTIVE REASONING is a process that begins with being able to identify instantly the fallacies of other forms of reasoning.

Deductive Reasoning is *always* accurate and as such it is the most effective tool for Critical Thinking.

Deductive Reasoning is the best way to make the decisions for:

+ analyzing and explaining risks
+ designing & implementing initiatives
+ allocating resources
+ anticipating & preventing errors
+ analyzing markets
+ using & managing information systems
+ assessing opportunities & competition
+ evaluating the effects of initiatives
+ identifying & analyzing emergent concerns
+ developing data security protocols
+ evolving long term goals and plans
+ communicating effectively with team members
+ evaluating customer service
+ anticipating the implications of actions taken
+ hiring and promoting leaders

- + analyzing and resolving personnel issues
- + explaining policy and procedures
- + designing & evaluating departmental reports
  ... and many other key decisions.

Most interestingly, the mistakes of both *abductive* and *inductive* reasoning are easily and quickly avoidable if we learn to instantly recognize them.

Moreover, once we learn to recognize those mistakes, truly object deductive reasoning becomes *very* easy.

There are 18 common fallacies that lead to the incorrect conclusions of non-deductive reasoning.

If we learn to identify them, then we are well on the road to effective reasoning for our business.

The 18 most-common logical fallacies that get in the way of deductive reasoning:
As improbable as it sounds, it is true that we can almost instantly discard non-deductive conclusions once we can recognize these most-common decision-making failures.

There is no shortcut to the technique. We simply have to learn to recognize these 18 mistakes.

FALLACY	Why It Is Not DEDUCTIVE
Appeal to force	Exactly what it sounds like; a threat.
Abuse	Attacking the messenger rather the message; not arguing the issue but arguing about the person who presented the issue.
Circumstantial	Example: You should buy an American-made car not because of the merits of the vehicle but because to buy a foreign car would be "un-American" or against the tenets of being a good citizen.
Argument from ignorance	This is an argument that is said to be true just because no one has ever proven it is not true. For example, "there must be ghosts because no one has proven there are no ghosts."
Appeal to pity	Exactly what it sounds like
Bandwagon	Emotional appeal "to the people." You should smoke a certain brand of cigarettes because it will give you sex appeal; drink a certain kind of beer will make you have fun in a bar like the guys in the commercial. Advertisements use this fallacy subliminally by depicting happy people in expensive surroundings using their product ... implying that

FALLACY	Why It Is Not DEDUCTIVE
	if you use the product you will be part of that life-style.
Appeal to authority	... or and expert opinion, without regard to other factors.
Accidental circumstances	This occurs when one applies a general rule to a specific case and implies that the general rule is universally true without exception. The VGT example, previously.
Hasty Generalization	If you take several "exceptions" to a general rule and claim that they are the rule, you commit this fallacy. For example: 100 people who had sex got AIDS; therefore no one should ever have sex.
Negative correlations	My favorite example of this fallacy is the famous situation involving the New York City newspapers following the power blackout of 1964. In May of 1965, nine months after the blackout, reporters noticed an increase in the birth rate in the city. The papers announced that this was because without electricity, television and lights on those fateful three days nine months earlier couples had nothing better to do than make whoopee...and hence the baby boom. It was later that it was discovered that the birth rate increases every year during May and in 1965 the figures were actually down from the previous May's increase. Another example I often give of this fallacy is consideration of the relationship between shoe size and vocabulary in children. Between kindergarten and 10th grade a child's shoe sizes get larger. So, does her/his vocabulary. Therefore, the bigger the shoes the bigger the vocabulary. Such is a fallacy.
Begging the question or Circular argument	When presenting the conclusion of an argument as a premise, one is begging the question. For example: You might argue that Sunday morning worship service at the local church is attended by good people. And if I were to ask what makes these people "good," you would respond, "they attend Sunday morning worship service."
Complex question	"Do you still beat your spouse?", is the typical example of this fallacy. The conclusion is implied in the question. If you say "yes," then you admit that you beat your spouse; but if you say "no" you still

FALLACY	Why It Is Not DEDUCTIVE
	admit that you did at one time beat your spouse, but you are not still doing it.
Irrelevant conclusion	Example: "If we want to avoid being overrun by terrorist nations, we must develop an adequate defense capability. So, it follows that we must deploy a Neutron bomb system and the MX missile system." This is a fallacy because the Neutron bomb and the MX system are offensive weapons and do not relate to defense in any way. The conclusion is irrelevant to the premise of defense.
Equivocation	Many words in the English language have more than one meaning. An equivocation is an ambiguous use of words. For example: "It is our duty to do what is right. We have the right to disregard good advice. Hence, it is our duty to disregard good advice." The equivocation involves the dual meanings of the word "right."
Amphiboly	This is another grammatical error. One of my favorite examples is: "I've looked in every bookstore in town for a step-by-step beginner's instruction book on how to play the piano without success." Obviously, from this sentence structure I am looking for a book about "how to play the piano without success."
Accent	This is another shift-in-meaning fallacy which is dependent on how the statement is accented. One of my favorite examples comes from a headline I put on the front page of a union newspaper several years ago. Five union members (out of a total of 42,000) were tested for asbestos poisoning. Of those five, four of them were determined to be poisoned. My headline screamed at the readers: "FOUR OUT OF FIVE UNION MEMBERS POISONED ON THE JOB." Reading it one way was absolutely true...but my accident left open an entirely different meaning.
Composition or Specific-to-Universal	This relates to putting sentence together so that it is misleading. For example: "In the new FORD, the heaviest single part of the car weighs only 35 pounds...and that is the driver's seat. Therefore, the new FORD is extremely light weight." This is not necessarily true because even if every other

FALLACY	Why It Is Not DEDUCTIVE
	part only weighs one-pound, there may be 450,000 parts giving the car a weight of 450,000+ pounds. But the sentence is structured to mislead.
Division or Universal-to-Specific	This is the opposite of the composition fallacy; that what is true of a whole must be true of its parts. For example: "Americans love hot dogs. I am an American. Therefore, I love hot dogs." The fact is, I am a vegetarian and I despise hot dogs. This fallacy is also fun to use in parody: "Men who wear hats are vanishing. That man is wearing a hat. Therefore, that man is vanishing."

WHY?

Once we are armed with the ability to identify these logical fallacies, it is only a matter of looking at every decision and asking if our conclusion comes from one of those or is it truly deduction from the facts.

That is easily accomplished by repeatedly asking "why" about every decision.

Once we ask "why", we then ask "why" at least four more times.

Wikipedia, the online encyclopedia, explains this "why" process with the example of a car failing to start:

1. **WHY** won't it start? *The battery is dead.* (First why)

2. **WHY** is the battery dead? *The alternator is not functioning.* (Second why)

3. **WHY** is the alternator not working? *The alternator belt has broken.* (Third why)

4. **WHY** is the belt broken? *The alternator belt was well beyond its useful service life and not replaced.* (Fourth why)

5. **WHY** was it not replaced? *The vehicle was not maintained according to the recommended service schedule.* (Fifth why, a root cause)

This method of reasoning is often called *The Rule of Five Whys*. It was created in the late 19th century by Sakichi Toyoda, the founder of Toyota Automobiles (which became the sixth largest company in the world).

Mr. Toyoda used the technique as a way to get to the root cause of manufacturing problems. But beyond manufacturing, the technique proved so successful that the it was adopted into the twentieth century business process systems *Six Sigma* and *Kaizen*.

In the 21st century, we have applied the *"Five Whys"* as a series of steps to gather data and begin the critical thinking process.

This allows us to apply deductive reasoning, rather than make abductive or inductive decisions.

It gives us the ability to analyze the collected data to make strategic decisions, provide sound planning, and create effective operations. It all begins with repeatedly asking "Why".

Therein is Alice and the Cheshire Cat's starting point for Strategic Planning.

The process is made up of five steps (vision, mission, objectives, strategies, and action plans). Each of those steps begins with the process of Critical Thinking. And, the Critical Thinking process requires deductive reasoning, which is fueled by the five "Whys".

Together, this lays the groundwork for implementing the processes described in the *Planning* chapter of this book.

Willapa Bay; the home of the Shoalwater Bay Tribe

ABOVE: Johnny Winokur at home on a casino floor. BELOW **LEFT:** Mike Rasmussen supervises moving the breeding pools for the WBE oyster farm. **BELOW RIGHT:** Rasmussen checks the chemical trays for the process.

endnotes

1 The current list of "recognized" Tribes according to the 2018 Federal Register:

- Absentee-Shawnee Tribe of Indians of Oklahoma
- Agdaagux Tribe of King Cove
- Agua Caliente Band of Cahuilla Indians of the Agua Caliente Indian Reservation, California
- Ak-Chin Indian Community (previously listed as the Ak Chin Indian Community of the Maricopa (Ak Chin) Indian Reservation, Arizona)
- Akiachak Native Community
- Akiak Native Community
- Alabama-Coushatta Tribe of Texas (previously listed as the Alabama-Coushatta Tribes of Texas)
- Alabama-Quassarte Tribal Town
- Alatna Village
- Algaaciq Native Village (St. Mary's)
- Allakaket Village
- Alturas Indian Rancheria, California
- Alutiiq Tribe of Old Harbor (previously listed as Native Village of Old Harbor and Village of Old Harbor)
- Angoon Community Association
- Native Village of Napaskiak
- Native Village of Nelson Lagoon
- Native Village of Nightmute
- Native Village of Nikolski
- Native Village of Noatak
- Native Village of Nuiqsut (aka Nooiksut)
- Native Village of Nunam Iqua (previously listed as the Native Village of Sheldon's Point)
- Native Village of Nunapitchuk
- Native Village of Ouzinkie
- Native Village of Paimiut
- Native Village of Perryville
- Native Village of Pilot Point
- Native Village of Pitka's Point
- Native Village of Point Hope
- Native Village of Point Lay
- Native Village of Port Graham
- Native Village of Port Heiden
- Native Village of Port Lions
- Native Village of Ruby
- Native Village of Saint Michael
- Native Village of Savoonga

82

- Anvik Village
- Apache Tribe of Oklahoma
- Arapaho Tribe of the Wind River Reservation, Wyoming
- Arctic Village (See Native Village of Venetie Tribal Government)
- Aroostook Band of Micmacs (previously listed as the Aroostook Band of Micmac Indians)
- Asa'carsarmiut Tribe
- Assiniboine and Sioux Tribes of the Fort Peck Indian Reservation, Montana
- Atqasuk Village (Atkasook)
- Augustine Band of Cahuilla Indians, California (previously listed as the Augustine Band of Cahuilla Mission Indians of the Augustine Reservation)
- Bad River Band of the Lake Superior Tribe of Chippewa Indians of the Bad River Reservation, Wisconsin
- Bay Mills Indian Community, Michigan
- Bear River Band of the Rohnerville Rancheria, California
- Beaver Village
- Berry Creek Rancheria of Maidu Indians of California
- Big Lagoon Rancheria, California
- Native Village of Scammon Bay
- Native Village of Selawik
- Native Village of Shaktoolik
- Native Village of Shishmaref
- Native Village of Shungnak
- Native Village of Stevens
- Native Village of Tanacross
- Native Village of Tanana
- Native Village of Tatitlek
- Native Village of Tazlina
- Native Village of Teller
- Native Village of Tetlin
- Native Village of Tuntutuliak
- Native Village of Tununak
- Native Village of Tyonek
- Native Village of Unalakleet
- Native Village of Unga Native Village of Venetie Tribal Government (Arctic Village and Village of Venetie)
- Native Village of Wales
- Native Village of White Mountain
- Navajo Nation, Arizona, New Mexico & Utah
- Nenana Native Association
- New Koliganek Village Council
- New Stuyahok Village
- Newhalen Village
- Newtok Village

83

- Big Pine Paiute Tribe of the Owens Valley (previously listed as the Big Pine Band of Owens Valley Paiute Shoshone Indians of the Big Pine Reservation, California)
- Big Sandy Rancheria of Western Mono Indians of California (previously listed as the Big Sandy Rancheria of Mono Indians of California)
- Big Valley Band of Pomo Indians of the Big Valley Rancheria, California
- Birch Creek Tribe
- Bishop Paiute Tribe (previously listed as the Paiute-Shoshone Indians of the Bishop Community of the Bishop Colony, California)
- Blackfeet Tribe of the Blackfeet Indian Reservation of Montana
- Blue Lake Rancheria, California
- Bridgeport Indian Colony (previously listed as the Bridgeport Paiute Indian Colony of California)
- Buena Vista Rancheria of Me-Wuk Indians of California
- Burns Paiute Tribe (previously listed as the Burns Paiute Tribe of the Burns Paiute Indian Colony of Oregon)

- Nez Perce Tribe (previously listed as the Nez Perce Tribe of Idaho)
- Nikolai Village
- Ninilchik Village
- Nisqually Indian Tribe (previously listed as the Nisqually Indian Tribe of the Nisqually Reservation, Washington)
- Nome Eskimo Community
- Nondalton Village
- Nooksack Indian Tribe
- Noorvik Native Community
- Northern Cheyenne Tribe of the Northern Cheyenne Indian Reservation, Montana
- Northfork Rancheria of Mono Indians of California
- Northway Village
- Northwestern Band of Shoshoni Nation and the Northwestern Band of Shoshoni Nation of Utah (Washakie))
- Northwestern Band of the Shoshone Nation (previously listed as
- Nottawaseppi Huron Band of the Potawatomi, Michigan (previously listed as the Huron Potawatomi, Inc.)
- Nulato Village
- Nunakauyarmiut Tribe
- Oglala Sioux Tribe (previously listed as the Oglala Sioux Tribe of the Pine

- Cabazon Band of Mission Indians, California
- Cachil DeHe Band of Wintun Indians of the Colusa Indian Community of the Colusa Rancheria, California
- Caddo Nation of Oklahoma
- Cahto Tribe of the Laytonville Rancheria
- Cahuilla Band of Indians (previously listed as the Cahuilla Band of Mission Indians of the Cahuilla Reservation, California)
- California Valley Miwok Tribe, California
- Campo Band of Diegueno Mission Indians of the Campo Indian Reservation, California
- Capitan Grande Band of Diegueno Mission Indians of California (Barona Group of Capitan Grande Band of Mission Indians of the Barona Reservation, California;
- Catawba Indian Nation (aka Catawba Tribe of South Carolina)
- Cayuga Nation
- Cedarville Rancheria, California
- Central Council of the Tlingit & Haida Indian Tribes
- Chalkyitsik Village
- Cheesh-Na Tribe (previously listed as the Native Village of Chistochina)
- Ridge Reservation, South Dakota)
- Ohkay Owingeh, New Mexico (previously listed as the Pueblo of San Juan)
- Omaha Tribe of Nebraska
- Oneida Indian Nation (previously listed as the Oneida Nation of New York)
- Oneida Nation (previously listed as the Oneida Tribe of Indians of Wisconsin)
- Onondaga Nation
- Organized Village of Grayling (aka Holikachuk)
- Organized Village of Kake
- Organized Village of Kasaan
- Organized Village of Kwethluk
- Organized Village of Saxman
- Orutsararmiut Traditional Native Council (previously listed as Orutsararmuit Native Village (aka Bethel))
- Oscarville Traditional Village
- Otoe-Missouria Tribe of Indians, Oklahoma
- Ottawa Tribe of Oklahoma
- Paiute Indian Tribe of Utah (Cedar Band of Paiutes, Kanosh Band of Paiutes, Koosharem Band of Paiutes, Indian Peaks Band of Paiutes, and Shivwits Band of Paiutes (formerly Paiute Indian Tribe of Utah (Cedar

- Chemehuevi Indian Tribe of the Chemehuevi Reservation, California
- Cher-Ae Heights Indian Community of the Trinidad Rancheria, California
- Cherokee Nation
- Chevak Native Village
- Cheyenne and Arapaho Tribes, Oklahoma (previously listed as the Cheyenne-Arapaho Tribes of Oklahoma)
- Cheyenne River Sioux Tribe of the Cheyenne River Reservation, South Dakota
- Chickaloon Native Village
- Chicken Ranch Rancheria of Me-Wuk Indians of California
- Chignik Bay Tribal Council (previously listed as the Native Village of Chignik)
- Chignik Lake Village
- Chilkat Indian Village (Klukwan)
- Chilkoot Indian Association (Haines)
- Chinik Eskimo Community (Golovin)
- Chippewa Cree Indians of the Rocky Boy's Reservation, Montana (previously listed as the Chippewa-Cree Indians of the Rocky Boy's Reservation, Montana)
- Chitimacha Tribe of Louisiana

- City Band of Paiutes, Kanosh Band of Paiutes, Koosharem Band of Paiutes, Indian Peaks Band of Paiutes, and Shivwits Band of Paiutes))
- Paiute-Shoshone Tribe of the Fallon Reservation and Colony, Nevada
- Pala Band of Mission Indians (previously listed as the Pala Band of Luiseno Mission Indians of the Pala Reservation, California)
- Pamunkey Indian Tribe
- Pascua Yaqui Tribe of Arizona
- Paskenta Band of Nomlaki Indians of California
- Passamaquoddy Tribe
- Pauloff Harbor Village
- Pauma Band of Luiseno Mission Indians of the Pauma & Yuima Reservation, California
- Pawnee Nation of Oklahoma
- Pechanga Band of Luiseno Mission Indians of the Pechanga Reservation, California
- Pedro Bay Village
- Penobscot Nation (previously listed as the Penobscot Tribe of Maine)
- Peoria Tribe of Indians of Oklahoma
- Petersburg Indian Association

- Chuloonawick Native Village
- Circle Native Community
- Citizen Potawatomi Nation, Oklahoma
- Cloverdale Rancheria of Pomo Indians of California
- Cocopah Tribe of Arizona
- Coeur D'Alene Tribe (previously listed as the Coeur D'Alene Tribe of the Coeur D'Alene Reservation, Idaho)
- Cold Springs Rancheria of Mono Indians of California
- Colorado River Indian Tribes of the Colorado River Indian Reservation, Arizona and California
- Comanche Nation, Oklahoma
- Confederated Salish and Kootenai Tribes of the Flathead Reservation
- Confederated Tribes and Bands of the Yakama Nation
- Confederated Tribes of Siletz Indians of Oregon (previously listed as the Confederated Tribes of the Siletz Reservation)
- Confederated Tribes of the Chehalis Reservation
- Confederated Tribes of the Colville Reservation
- Confederated Tribes of the Coos, Lower Umpqua and Siuslaw Indians
- Picayune Rancheria of Chukchansi Indians of California
- Pilot Station Traditional Village
- Pinoleville Pomo Nation, California (previously listed as the Pinoleville Rancheria of Pomo Indians of California)
- Pit River Tribe, California (includes XL Ranch, Big Bend, Likely, Lookout, Montgomery Creek and Roaring Creek Rancherias)
- Platinum Traditional Village
- Poarch Band of Creeks (previously listed as the Poarch Band of Creek Indians of Alabama)
- Pokagon Band of Potawatomi Indians, Michigan and Indiana
- Ponca Tribe of Indians of Oklahoma
- Ponca Tribe of Nebraska
- Port Gamble S'Klallam Tribe (previously listed as the Port Gamble Band of S'Klallam Indians)
- Portage Creek Village (aka Ohgsenakale)
- Potter Valley Tribe, California
- Prairie Band Potawatomi Nation (previously listed as the Prairie Band of Potawatomi Nation, Kansas)

- Confederated Tribes of the Goshute Reservation, Nevada and Utah
- Confederated Tribes of the Grand Ronde Community of Oregon
- Confederated Tribes of the Umatilla Indian Reservation (previously listed as the Confederated Tribes of the Umatilla Reservation, Oregon)
- Confederated Tribes of the Warm Springs Reservation of Oregon
- Coquille Indian Tribe (previously listed as the Coquille Tribe of Oregon)
- Coushatta Tribe of Louisiana
- Cow Creek Band of Umpqua Tribe of Indians (previously listed as the Cow Creek Band of Umpqua Indians of Oregon)
- Cowlitz Indian Tribe
- Coyote Valley Band of Pomo Indians of California
- Craig Tribal Association (previously listed as the Craig Community Association)
- Crow Creek Sioux Tribe of the Crow Creek Reservation, South Dakota
- Crow Tribe of Montana
- Curyung Tribal Council
- Death Valley Timbi-sha Shoshone Tribe (previously

- Prairie Island Indian Community in the State of Minnesota
- Pribilof Islands Aleut Communities of St. Paul & St. George Islands
- Pueblo of Acoma, New Mexico
- Pueblo of Cochiti, New Mexico
- Pueblo of Isleta, New Mexico
- Pueblo of Jemez, New Mexico
- Pueblo of Laguna, New Mexico
- Pueblo of Nambe, New Mexico
- Pueblo of Picuris, New Mexico
- Pueblo of Pojoaque, New Mexico
- Pueblo of San Felipe, New Mexico
- Pueblo of San Ildefonso, New Mexico
- Pueblo of Sandia, New Mexico
- Pueblo of Santa Ana, New Mexico
- Pueblo of Santa Clara, New Mexico
- Pueblo of Taos, New Mexico
- Pueblo of Tesuque, New Mexico
- Pueblo of Zia, New Mexico
- Puyallup Tribe of the Puyallup Reservation

- listed as the Death Valley Timbi-Sha Shoshone Band of California)
- Delaware Nation, Oklahoma
- Delaware Tribe of Indians
- Douglas Indian Association
- Dry Creek Rancheria Band of Pomo Indians, California (previously listed as the Dry Creek Rancheria of Pomo Indians of California)
- Duckwater Shoshone Tribe of the Duckwater Reservation, Nevada
- Eastern Band of Cherokee Indians
- Eastern Shawnee Tribe of Oklahoma
- Eastern Shoshone Tribe of the Wind River Reservation, Wyoming (previously listed as the Shoshone Tribe of the Wind River Reservation, Wyoming)
- Egegik Village
- Eklutna Native Village
- Elem Indian Colony of Pomo Indians of the Sulphur Bank Rancheria, California
- Elk Valley Rancheria, California
- Ely Shoshone Tribe of Nevada
- Emmonak Village
- Enterprise Rancheria of Maidu Indians of California
- Evansville Village (aka Bettles Field)

- Pyramid Lake Paiute Tribe of the Pyramid Lake Reservation, Nevada
- Qagan Tayagungin Tribe of Sand Point Village
- Qawalangin Tribe of Unalaska
- Quartz Valley Indian Community of the Quartz Valley Reservation of California
- Quechan Tribe of the Fort Yuma Indian Reservation, California & Arizona
- Quileute Tribe of the Quileute Reservation
- Quinault Indian Nation (previously listed as the Quinault Tribe of the Quinault Reservation, Washington)
- Ramona Band of Cahuilla, California (previously listed as the Ramona Band or Village of Cahuilla Mission Indians of California)
- Rampart Village
- Red Cliff Band of Lake Superior Chippewa Indians of Wisconsin
- Red Lake Band of Chippewa Indians, Minnesota
- Redding Rancheria, California
- Redwood Valley or Little River Band of Pomo Indians of the Redwood Valley Rancheria California (pre-

- Ewiiaapaayp Band of Kumeyaay Indians, California
- Federated Indians of Graton Rancheria, California
- Flandreau Santee Sioux Tribe of South Dakota
- Forest County Potawatomi Community, Wisconsin
- Fort Belknap Indian Community of the Fort Belknap Reservation of Montana
- Fort Bidwell Indian Community of the Fort Bidwell Reservation of California
- Fort Independence Indian Community of Paiute Indians of the Fort Independence Reservation, California
- Fort McDermitt Paiute and Shoshone Tribes of the Fort McDermitt Indian Reservation, Nevada and Oregon
- Fort McDowell Yavapai Nation, Arizona
- Fort Mojave Indian Tribe of Arizona, California & Nevada
- Fort Sill Apache Tribe of Oklahoma
- Galena Village (aka Louden Village)
- Gila River Indian Community of the Gila River Indian Reservation, Arizona
- Grand Traverse Band of Ottawa and Chippewa Indians, Michigan
- viously listed as the Redwood Valley Rancheria of Pomo Indians of California)
- Reno-Sparks Indian Colony, Nevada
- Resighini Rancheria, California
- Rincon Band of Luiseno Mission Indians of the Rincon Reservation, California
- Robinson Rancheria (previously listed as the Robinson Rancheria Band of Pomo Indians, California and the Robinson Rancheria of Pomo Indians of California)
- Rosebud Sioux Tribe of the Rosebud Indian Reservation, South Dakota
- Round Valley Indian Tribes, Round Valley Reservation, California (previously listed as the Round Valley Indian Tribes of the Round Valley Reservation, California)
- Sac & Fox Nation of Missouri in Kansas and Nebraska
- Sac & Fox Nation, Oklahoma
- Sac & Fox Tribe of the Mississippi in Iowa
- Saginaw Chippewa Indian Tribe of Michigan
- Saint George Island (See Pribilof Islands Aleut Communities of St. Paul & St. George Islands)

- Greenville Rancheria (previously listed as the Greenville Rancheria of Maidu Indians of California)
- Grindstone Indian Rancheria of Wintun-Wailaki Indians of California
- Guidiville Rancheria of California
- Gulkana Village
- Habematolel Pomo of Upper Lake, California
- Hannahville Indian Community, Michigan
- Havasupai Tribe of the Havasupai Reservation, Arizona
- Healy Lake Village
- Ho-Chunk Nation of Wisconsin
- Hoh Indian Tribe (previously listed as the Hoh Indian Tribe of the Hoh Indian Reservation, Washington)
- Holy Cross Village
- Hoonah Indian Association
- Hoopa Valley Tribe, California
- Hopi Tribe of Arizona
- Hopland Band of Pomo Indians, California (formerly Hopland Band of Pomo Indians of the Hopland Rancheria, California)
- Houlton Band of Maliseet Indians
- Hualapai Indian Tribe of the Hualapai Indian Reservation, Arizona
- Saint Paul Island (See Pribilof Islands Aleut Communities of St. Paul & St. George Islands)
- Saint Regis Mohawk Tribe (previously listed as the St. Regis Band of Mohawk Indians of New York)
- Salt River Pima-Maricopa Indian Community of the Salt River Reservation, Arizona
- Samish Indian Nation (previously listed as the Samish Indian Tribe, Washington)
- San Carlos Apache Tribe of the San Carlos Reservation, Arizona
- San Juan Southern Paiute Tribe of Arizona
- San Manuel Band of Mission Indians, California (previously listed as the San Manual Band of Serrano Mission Indians of the San Manual Reservation)
- San Pasqual Band of Diegueno Mission Indians of California
- Santa Rosa Band of Cahuilla Indians, California (previously listed as the Santa Rosa Band of Cahuilla Mission Indians of the Santa Rosa Reservation)

91

- Hughes Village
- Huslia Village
- Hydaburg Cooperative Association
- Igiugig Village
- Iipay Nation of Santa Ysabel, California (previously listed as the Santa Ysabel Band of Diegueno Mission Indians of the Santa Ysabel Reservation)
- Inaja Band of Diegueno Mission Indians of the Inaja and Cosmit Reservation, California
- Inupiat Community of the Arctic Slope
- Ione Band of Miwok Indians of California
- Iowa Tribe of Kansas and Nebraska
- Iowa Tribe of Oklahoma
- Iqurmuit Traditional Council
- Ivanof Bay Tribe (previously listed as the Ivanoff Bay Tribe and the Ivanoff Bay Village)
- Jackson Band of Miwuk Indians (previously listed as the Jackson Rancheria of Me-Wuk Indians of California)
- Jamestown S'Klallam Tribe
- Jamul Indian Village of California
- Jena Band of Choctaw Indians
- Jicarilla Apache Nation, New Mexico
- Santa Rosa Indian Community of the Santa Rosa Rancheria, California
- Santa Ynez Band of Chumash Mission Indians of the Santa Ynez Reservation, California
- Santee Sioux Nation, Nebraska
- Sauk-Suiattle Indian Tribe
- Sault Ste. Marie Tribe of Chippewa Indians, Michigan
- Scotts Valley Band of Pomo Indians of California
- Seldovia Village Tribe
- Seminole Tribe of Florida (previously listed as the Seminole Tribe of Florida (Dania, Big Cypress, Brighton, Hollywood & Tampa Reservations))
- Seneca Nation of Indians (previously listed as the Seneca Nation of New York)
- Seneca—Cayuga Nation (previously listed as the Seneca-Cayuga Tribe of Oklahoma)
- Shageluk Native Village
- Shakopee Mdewakanton Sioux Community of Minnesota
- Shawnee Tribe
- Sherwood Valley Rancheria of Pomo Indians of California
- Shingle Springs Band of Miwok Indians, Shingle

- Kaguyak Village
- Kaibab Band of Paiute Indians of the Kaibab Indian Reservation, Arizona
- Kaktovik Village (aka Barter Island)
- Kalispel Indian Community of the Kalispel Reservation
- Karuk Tribe (previously listed as the Karuk Tribe of California)
- Kashia Band of Pomo Indians of the Stewarts Point Rancheria, California
- Kasigluk Traditional Elders Council
- Kaw Nation, Oklahoma
- Kenaitze Indian Tribe
- Ketchikan Indian Corporation
- Kewa Pueblo, New Mexico (previously listed as the Pueblo of Santo Domingo)
- Keweenaw Bay Indian Community, Michigan
- Kialegee Tribal Town
- Kickapoo Traditional Tribe of Texas
- Kickapoo Tribe of Indians of the Kickapoo Reservation in Kansas
- Kickapoo Tribe of Oklahoma
- King Island Native Community
- King Salmon Tribe
- Kiowa Indian Tribe of Oklahoma
- Klamath Tribes

Springs Rancheria (Verona Tract), California
- Shinnecock Indian Nation
- **Shoalwater Bay Indian Tribe of the Shoalwater Bay Indian Reservation (previously listed as the Shoalwater Bay Tribe of the Shoalwater Bay Indian Reservation, Washington)**
- Shoshone-Bannock Tribes of the Fort Hall Reservation
- Shoshone-Paiute Tribes of the Duck Valley Reservation, Nevada
- Sisseton-Wahpeton Oyate of the Lake Traverse Reservation, South Dakota
- Sitka Tribe of Alaska
- Skagway Village
- Skokomish Indian Tribe (previously listed as the Skokomish Indian Tribe of the Skokomish Reservation, Washington)
- Skull Valley Band of Goshute Indians of Utah
- Snoqualmie Indian Tribe (previously listed as the Snoqualmie Tribe, Washington)
- Soboba Band of Luiseno Indians, California
- Sokaogon Chippewa Community, Wisconsin
- South Naknek Village
- Southern Ute Indian Tribe of the Southern Ute Reservation, Colorado

- Klawock Cooperative Association
- Kletsel Dehe Band of Wintun Indians (previously listed as the Cortina Indian Rancheria and the Cortina Indian Rancheria of Wintun Indians of California)
- Knik Tribe
- Koi Nation of Northern California (previously listed as the Lower Lake Rancheria, California)
- Kokhanok Village
- Kootenai Tribe of Idaho
- Koyukuk Native Village
- La Jolla Band of Luiseno Indians, California (previously listed as the La Jolla Band of Luiseno Mission Indians of the La Jolla Reservation)
- La Posta Band of Diegueno Mission Indians of the La Posta Indian Reservation, California
- Lac Courte Oreilles Band of Lake Superior Chippewa Indians of Wisconsin
- Lac du Flambeau Band of Lake Superior Chippewa Indians of the Lac du Flambeau Reservation of Wisconsin
- Lac Vieux Desert Band of Lake Superior Chippewa Indians of Michigan
- Las Vegas Tribe of Paiute Indians of the Las Vegas Indian Colony, Nevada
- Spirit Lake Tribe, North Dakota
- Spokane Tribe of the Spokane Reservation
- Squaxin Island Tribe of the Squaxin Island Reservation
- St. Croix Chippewa Indians of Wisconsin
- Standing Rock Sioux Tribe of North & South Dakota
- Stebbins Community Association
- Stillaguamish Tribe of Indians of Washington (previously listed as the Stillaguamish Tribe of Washington)
- Stockbridge Munsee Community, Wisconsin
- Summit Lake Paiute Tribe of Nevada
- Sun'aq Tribe of Kodiak (previously listed as the Shoonaq' Tribe of Kodiak)
- Suquamish Indian Tribe of the Port Madison Reservation
- Susanville Indian Rancheria, California
- Swinomish Indian Tribal Community (previously listed as the Swinomish Indians of the Swinomish Reservation of Washington)
- Sycuan Band of the Kumeyaay Nation
- Table Mountain Rancheria (previously listed as the

- Levelock Village
- Lime Village
- Little River Band of Ottawa Indians, Michigan
- Little Traverse Bay Bands of Odawa Indians, Michigan
- Lone Pine Paiute-Shoshone Tribe (previously listed as the Paiute-Shoshone Indians of the Lone Pine Community of the Lone Pine Reservation, California)
- Los Coyotes Band of Cahuilla and Cupeno Indians, California (previously listed as the Los Coyotes Band of Cahuilla & Cupeno Indians of the Los Coyotes Reservation)
- Lovelock Paiute Tribe of the Lovelock Indian Colony, Nevada
- Lower Brule Sioux Tribe of the Lower Brule Reservation, South Dakota
- Lower Elwha Tribal Community (previously listed as the Lower Elwha Tribal Community of the Lower Elwha Reservation, Washington)
- Lower Sioux Indian Community in the State of Minnesota
- Lummi Tribe of the Lummi Reservation
- Lytton Rancheria of California

- Table Mountain Rancheria of California)
- Takotna Village
- Tangirnaq Native Village (formerly Lesnoi Village (aka Woody Island))
- Tejon Indian Tribe
- Telida Village
- Te-Moak Tribe of Western Shoshone Indians of Nevada (Four constituent bands: Battle Mountain Band; Elko Band; South Fork Band and Wells Band)
- The Chickasaw Nation
- The Choctaw Nation of Oklahoma
- The Modoc Tribe of Oklahoma
- The Muscogee (Creek) Nation
- The Osage Nation (previously listed as the Osage Tribe)
- The Quapaw Tribe of Indians
- The Seminole Nation of Oklahoma
- Thlopthlocco Tribal Town
- Three Affiliated Tribes of the Fort Berthold Reservation, North Dakota
- Tohono O'odham Nation of Arizona
- Tolowa Dee-ni' Nation (previously listed as the Smith River Rancheria, California)
- Tonawanda Band of Seneca (previously listed as

- Makah Indian Tribe of the Makah Indian Reservation
- Manchester Band of Pomo Indians of the Manchester Rancheria, California (previously listed as the Manchester Band of Pomo Indians of the Manchester-Point Arena Rancheria, California)
- Manley Hot Springs Village
- Manokotak Village
- Manzanita Band of Diegueno Mission Indians of the Manzanita Reservation, California
- Mashantucket Pequot Indian Tribe (previously listed as the Mashantucket Pequot Tribe of Connecticut)
- Mashpee Wampanoag Tribe (previously listed as the Mashpee Wampanoag Indian Tribal Council, Inc.)
- Match-e-be-nash-she-wish Band of Pottawatomi Indians of Michigan
- McGrath Native Village
- Mechoopda Indian Tribe of Chico Rancheria, California
- Menominee Indian Tribe of Wisconsin
- Mentasta Traditional Council
- Mesa Grande Band of Diegueno Mission Indians of the Mesa Grande Reservation, California
- the Tonawanda Band of Seneca Indians of New York)
- Tonkawa Tribe of Indians of Oklahoma
- Tonto Apache Tribe of Arizona
- Torres Martinez Desert Cahuilla Indians, California (previously listed as the Torres-Martinez Band of Cahuilla Mission Indians of California)
- Traditional Village of Togiak
- Tulalip Tribes of Washington (previously listed as the Tulalip Tribes of the Tulalip Reservation, Washington)
- Tule River Indian Tribe of the Tule River Reservation, California
- Tuluksak Native Community
- Tunica-Biloxi Indian Tribe
- Tuolumne Band of Me-Wuk Indians of the Tuolumne Rancheria of California
- Turtle Mountain Band of Chippewa Indians of North Dakota
- Tuscarora Nation
- Twenty-Nine Palms Band of Mission Indians of California
- Twin Hills Village
- Ugashik Village

- Mescalero Apache Tribe of the Mescalero Reservation, New Mexico
- Metlakatla Indian Community, Annette Island Reserve
- Miami Tribe of Oklahoma
- Miccosukee Tribe of Indians
- Middletown Rancheria of Pomo Indians of California
- Minnesota Chippewa Tribe, Minnesota (Six component reservations: Bois Forte Band (Nett Lake); Fond du Lac Band; Grand Portage Band; Leech Lake Band; Mille Lacs Band; White Earth Band)
- Mississippi Band of Choctaw Indians
- Moapa Band of Paiute Indians of the Moapa River Indian Reservation, Nevada
- Mohegan Tribe of Indians of Connecticut (previously listed as Mohegan Indian Tribe of Connecticut)
- Mooretown Rancheria of Maidu Indians of California
- Morongo Band of Mission Indians, California (previously listed as the Morongo Band of Cahuilla Mission Indians of the Morongo Reservation)
- Muckleshoot Indian Tribe (previously listed as the Muckleshoot Indian Tribe

- Umkumiut Native Village (previously listed as Umkumiute Native Village)
- United Auburn Indian Community of the Auburn Rancheria of California
- United Keetoowah Band of Cherokee Indians in Oklahoma
- Upper Sioux Community, Minnesota
- Upper Skagit Indian Tribe
- Ute Indian Tribe of the Uintah & Ouray Reservation, Utah
- Ute Mountain Ute Tribe (previously listed as the Ute Mountain Tribe of the Ute Mountain Reservation, Colorado, New Mexico & Utah)
- Utu Utu Gwaitu Paiute Tribe of the Benton Paiute Reservation, California
- Viejas (Baron Long) Group of Capitan Grande Band of Mission Indians of the Viejas Reservation, California)
- Village of Alakanuk
- Village of Anaktuvuk Pass
- Village of Aniak
- Village of Atmautluak
- Village of Bill Moore's Slough
- Village of Chefornak
- Village of Clarks Point
- Village of Crooked Creek
- Village of Dot Lake
- Village of Iliamna

- of the Muckleshoot Reservation, Washington)
- Naknek Native Village
- Narragansett Indian Tribe
- Native Village of Afognak
- Native Village of Akhiok
- Native Village of Akutan
- Native Village of Aleknagik
- Native Village of Ambler
- Native Village of Atka
- Native Village of Barrow Inupiat Traditional Government
- Native Village of Belkofski
- Native Village of Brevig Mission
- Native Village of Buckland
- Native Village of Cantwell
- Native Village of Chenega (aka Chanega)
- Native Village of Chignik Lagoon
- Native Village of Chitina
- Native Village of Chuathbaluk (Russian Mission, Kuskokwim)
- Native Village of Council
- Native Village of Deering
- Native Village of Diomede (aka Inalik)
- Native Village of Eagle
- Native Village of Eek
- Native Village of Ekuk
- Native Village of Ekwok (previously listed as Ekwok Village)
- Native Village of Elim
- Native Village of Eyak (Cordova)
- Village of Kalskag
- Village of Kaltag
- Village of Kotlik
- Village of Lower Kalskag
- Village of Ohogamiut
- Village of Red Devil
- Village of Salamatoff
- Village of Sleetmute
- Village of Solomon
- Village of Stony River
- Village of Venetie (See Native Village of Venetie Tribal Government)
- Village of Wainwright
- Walker River Paiute Tribe of the Walker River Reservation, Nevada
- Wampanoag Tribe of Gay Head (Aquinnah)
- Washoe Tribe of Nevada & California (Carson Colony, Dresslerville Colony, Woodfords Community, Stewart Community & Washoe Ranches)
- White Mountain Apache Tribe of the Fort Apache Reservation, Arizona
- Wichita and Affiliated Tribes (Wichita, Keechi, Waco & Tawakonie), Oklahoma
- Wilton Rancheria, California
- Winnebago Tribe of Nebraska
- Winnemucca Indian Colony of Nevada

- Native Village of False Pass
- Native Village of Fort Yukon
- Native Village of Gakona
- Native Village of Gambell
- Native Village of Georgetown
- Native Village of Goodnews Bay
- Native Village of Hamilton
- Native Village of Hooper Bay
- Native Village of Kanatak
- Native Village of Karluk
- Native Village of Kiana
- Native Village of Kipnuk
- Native Village of Kivalina
- Native Village of Kluti Kaah (aka Copper Center)
- Native Village of Kobuk
- Native Village of Kongiganak
- Native Village of Kotzebue
- Native Village of Koyuk
- Native Village of Kwigillingok
- Native Village of Kwinhagak (aka Quinhagak)
- Native Village of Larsen Bay
- Native Village of Marshall (aka Fortuna Ledge)
- Native Village of Mary's Igloo
- Native Village of Mekoryuk
- Native Village of Minto
- Native Village of Nanwalek (aka English Bay)

- Wiyot Tribe, California (previously listed as the Table Bluff Reservation—Wiyot Tribe)
- Wrangell Cooperative Association
- Wyandotte Nation
- Yakutat Tlingit Tribe
- Yankton Sioux Tribe of South Dakota
- Yavapai-Apache Nation of the Camp Verde Indian Reservation, Arizona
- Yavapai-Prescott Indian Tribe (previously listed as the Yavapai-Prescott Tribe of the Yavapai Reservation, Arizona)
- Yerington Paiute Tribe of the Yerington Colony & Campbell Ranch, Nevada
- Yocha Dehe Wintun Nation, California (previously listed as the Rumsey Indian Rancheria of Wintun Indians of California)
- Yomba Shoshone Tribe of the Yomba Reservation, Nevada
- Ysleta del Sur Pueblo (previously listed as the Ysleta Del Sur Pueblo of Texas)
- Yupiit of Andreafski
- Yurok Tribe of the Yurok Reservation, California
- Zuni Tribe of the Zuni Reservation, New Mexico
- Native Village of Napakiak
- Native Village of Napaimut

[2] "Manifest Destiny" is the 19th century doctrine that the white United States settlers were destined by God to expand across North America.

[3] Another 42,000 Native Americans served in the Vietnam War

[4] CONCURRENT RESOLUTION OF THE EIGHTY---THIRD CONGRESS, FIRST SESSION, 1953
August 1, 1953 | [H. Con. Res. 108] 67 Stat. B122

Whereas it is the policy of Congress, as rapidly as possible, to make the Indians within the territorial limits of the United States subject to the same laws and entitled to the same privileges and responsibilities as are applicable to other citizens of the United States, to end their status as wards of the United States, and to grant them all of the rights and prerogatives pertaining to American citizenship; and

Whereas the Indians within the territorial limits of the United States should assume their full responsibilities as American citizens:

Now, therefore, be it *Resolved by the House of Representatives (the Senate concurring),*

That it is declared to be the sense of Congress that, at the earliest possible time, all of the Indian tribes and the individual members thereof located within the States of California, Florida, New York, and Texas, and all of the following named Indian tribes and individual members thereof, should be freed from Federal supervision and control and from all disabilities and limitations specially applicable to Indians: The Flathead Tribe of Montana, the Klamath Tribe of Oregon, the Menominee Tribe of Wisconsin, the Potowatamie Tribe of Kansas and Nebraska, and those members of the Chippewa Tribe who are on the Turtle Mountain Reservation, North Dakota. It is further declared to be the sense of Congress that, upon the release of such tribes and individual members thereof from such disabilities and limitations, all offices of the Bureau of Indian Affairs in the States of California, Florida, New York, and Texas and all other offices of the Bureau of Indian Affairs whose primary purpose was to serve any Indian tribe or individual Indian freed from Federal supervision should be abolished. It is further declared to be the sense of Congress that the Secretary of the Interior should examine all existing legislation dealing with such Indians, and treaties between the Government of the United States and each such tribe, and report to Congress at the earliest practicable date, but not later than January 1, 1954, his recommendations for such legislation as, in his judgment, may be necessary to accomplish the purposes of this resolution.

Passed August 1, 1953.

5

[6] Vine Deloria Jr., *Indians of the Pacific Northwest* (Golden Colorado: Doubleday and Company, 19777), pp 55.

[7] Ibid, p p60

[8] James Gilchrist Swan, *The Northwest Coast, or Three Year's Residence in Washington Territory* (New York, Harper, 1857; reprinted by University of Washington Press, Seattle, 1969) pp 34

[9] United States v. McGowan, 2 F. Supp. 426 (W.D. Wash. 1931)

[10] Sam Howe Verhovek, *Mysterious Force Attacks Small Western Tribe's Young in the Womb* (The New York Times, March 26, 2000) online archives

[11] https://www.gpo.gov/fdsys/pkg/STATUTE-98/pdf/STATUTE-98-Pg1671.pdf
[12] Ibid

[13] Jonathan Taylor, "Good Corporate Governance for Tribal Enterprises," Reservation Economic Summit 2005, Developing your Political, Legal, and Corporate Infrastructure (February 8, 2005), p. 6.

[14] For a sample charter document, contact: info@GaryGreenGaming.com

[15] Gary Green, *Osceola's Revenge —the phenomena of Indian casinos* (Brick Tower Press, New York, March 2017) pp 38-39

[16] The Indian Gaming Regulatory Act (IGRA) defined three classes of games which significantly differ in Tribal, State, and Federal regulatory requirements.
CLASS I games are defined as "social games played solely for prizes of minimal value or traditional forms of Indian gaming engaged in by individuals as part of, or in connection with, tribal ceremonies or celebrations." Regulation of these games is strictly by the Tribe and not by either State or Federal governments.
CLASS II games, "includes bingo, related activities, and certain non-house-banked card games". Class II games are regulated by the Tribe under certain Federal guidelines.
CLASS III gaming is defined as "all forms of gaming that are not Class II gaming or Class II gaming". To engage in Class III games, a Tribe must enter into a Compact (agreement) with the State (and the State may tax the games or revenue; something they cannot do with Class II games).
[17] https://www.nigc.gov/images/uploads/enforcement-actions/SA-NOV-CO_99-10_Shoalwater_Bay_Indian_Tribe.pdf
[18] http://washington.casinocity.com/tokeland/shoalwater-bay-casino/map/nearest/

[19] Publication 3908 - Gaming Tax Law for Indian Tribal Governments; https://www.irs.gov/pub/irs-pdf/p3908.pdf

[20] The normal 24-hour period that any casino uses for accounting and business reporting

[21] This is a draft-copy of FinCEN Form 112

[22] Spacey, S. 2015. Crab Mentality, Cyberbullying and "Name and Shame" Rankings. In Press, Waikato University, New Zealand.

About the Author

Gary Green is one of the country's leading casino developers, operators, and marketers as well as the much-publicized star of the under-development network television series "*Casino Rescue*" and is one of the most written-about figures in modern casino gaming.

A former vice president of *Trump Hotels & Casino Resorts*, during the past 40 years Gary Green, himself, has become one of the casino industry's iconic brands and has worked in or managed almost every operating department inside a modern casino hotel resort.

Primarily known for his cutting-edge marketing technologies and creative programs, he also is widely-recognized as one of the casino world's most knowledgeable executives in every aspect of operations, strategic planning, and business modeling.

Just in the past year he has been quoted in *The New York Times, The Boston Globe, The Newark Star-Ledger, The Los Angeles Times, CNBC, Bloomberg, Yahoo Finance,* the official *NASDAQ* news feed, countless trade publications, and scores of syndicated and local radio and television news programs.

As Chairman of the luminary-filled Gary Green Gaming™ team of industry professionals, he is currently leading casino acquisitions, development, and rehab projects all across the country.

Gary Green™ is one of only a few casino executives colorful enough to be memorialized in the prestigious *Smithsonian Institution,* have thousands of *Twitter* followers and *Facebook* fans, registered in *IMDB.com* (Internet Movie Database), listed in the *Wikipedia* online encyclopedia, and have two *Pulitzer Prize* nominations, along with a string of other honors and awards.

He has spent more than four decades in the casino and entertainment industry in roles from marketing to CEO.

He has served on the Board of Directors of the publicly-traded *Atlantis Internet Group*; on the board of the Las Vegas based *Association of Gaming Equipment Manufacturers* (AGEM); on the Board of privately-held *Hotel Smart Rooms, Inc.*, and of *Tenare Record Corporation*; and he is the former owner of the world-renowned *EuroCircus*.

Follow Gary Green on Social Media

www.GaryGreen.com

Other Works by Gary Green

available from

amazon   BARNES&NOBLE   ...and other fine book sellers
BOOKSELLERS

Osceola's Revenge — The Phenomena of Indian Casinos • Brick Tower Press • from an Amazon reviewer: *"This book presents a mostly unknown history of the creation of Native American Casinos. Find out how they work and the issues they have had to deal with. Gary Green is a very knowledgeable casino innovator and historian presenting a subject he has been deeply involved in. His experience includes being a GM of several Native American owned casinos including being on one of Trumps casino management teams. Very interesting read."*

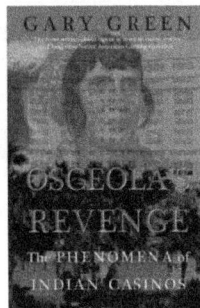

Crossroaders, Georges, & Sporting Men

"This biography covers the exhilarating life of one of the most colorful and interest-ing casino bosses ever: Gary Green." — **Carbon Poker**

"If you want to know about casinos and the gaming business, you go to one guy, and that guy is Gary Green." — **David Weischadle, House of Cards:**

Terrence Nash, ADI News: "A no-holds barred depiction of Green's escapades in the world of casino operations, dating as far back as the last days of Meyer Lansky's gambling empire up to the author's stint as a Donald Trump casino marketing executive. After all, Gary Green is well recognized as a seasoned casino manager who practices his profession by utilizing business analytics, risk assessments, predictive modeling and up-and-coming technologies in improving the organization, funding and performance of modern casino businesses."

4th & 30: When Journalism Counted

A roman à clef novelization is a novel about real life, overlaid with a façade of fiction.

It is real. It Happened. And it mattered.
There used to be something called JOURNALISM. It was a noble "Fourth Estate". There was no concept of anything called "fake news". Cronkite was the "most trusted man in America" and the Times & Post were paragons of integrity. Newspapers were actually "a thing".

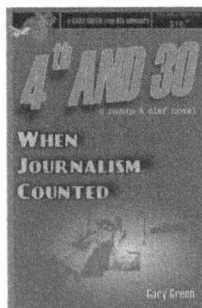

In a city with the highest per-capita murder rate in the country, Gary Green often arrived on the scene before the cops. Known for unorthodox hands-on reporting that took readers into and behind the scenes, his life was filled with shoot-outs, drug raids, high-speed chases, and every manner of blood and gore. His colorful exploits led to an international mystery of entanglements that made Moriarty look like a piker.

OTHER TITLES:

Gambling Man
Pay No Attention To The Man Behind The Curtain
Marketing-Driven Casino Operational Business Plan
Marketing Donald Trump

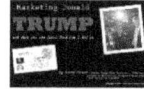

Gary Green's three legendary albums originally recorded for the highly-prestigious Folkways Records but re-released by the Smithsonian Institution in Washington DC. Available directly from the Smithsonian or from Amazon, iTunes Store, and other music markets. *These Six Strings Neutralize The Tools Of Oppression* (1976); *Allegory* (1977); *Still At Large* (1980). http://www.folkways.si.edu/search/Gary-Green